Thinking About Religion

Peter Mullen

Hodder & Stoughton
LONDON SYDNEY AUCKLAND TORONTO

British Library Cataloguing in Publication Data

Mullen, Peter
  Thinking about Religion
  1. Theology, Doctrinal — Study and teaching (secondary)
  I. Title
  230'.07'12   BV1471.2
  ISBN 0 7131 0468 6

First published in 1980
Seventh impression 1991

Printed in Great Britain for the educational publishing division of
Hodder and Stoughton Ltd, Mill Road, Dunton Green, Sevenoaks,
Kent by Athenaeum Press Ltd, Newcastle upon Tyne.

Preface

The trouble with trying to teach religion is deciding what to teach. I suppose the same holds true in most other subjects but not to such an exaggerated extent as it does in R. E. So questions arise: should we teach the Bible? Should we teach world Faiths? What about morality, church history and modern ideologies of all shades? In fact, should we teach anything at all? Perhaps we should stand back and let R. E. fade away? It doesn't seem to have much to do with the world today.

These problems present themselves because of the crisis of faith produced by the rise of science and secularism in the nineteenth and twentieth centuries. Unfortunately for R. E. much of our progress in these areas has led first to confusion and then to dogmatism among many — including some teachers and (dare I say it?) even including some who teach the teachers. Dogmatism is the ideal prescription for divisiveness. And divisiveness causes a stagnant feud.

Apart from the dictates of the 'O' and 'A' level syllabuses there are three widespread approaches to R. E. in the secondary school.

First, there are still those minority of extremists — fundamentalists who hold that every word of the Bible is 'God breathed' and must be accepted without question. There are the enthusiastic evangelicals who reject all the insights of biblical criticism. Personally, I am glad that they are a minority and could hope that this minority might be further reduced. Fundamentalism is the 'head in the sand' approach to R. E. Although it can easily be disproved — e.g. by showing that two biblical accounts describe the same event differently — it persists through the enthusiasm of its adherents to make the whole of R. E. seem incredible to many.

Secondly, there is the world Faiths approach: Hinduism, Islam, Buddhism, etc. Given our multicultural society it is no doubt useful to know something of these faiths, but I believe that it justifies its educational rationale only at the expense of theological honesty. For it can so easily become a way of dodging basic religious issues — in particular the problem of God's existence — and settle for colourful descriptivism. In the old days St Paul's journeys provided the same escape route by allowing the teacher to talk about geography, anthropology (and even techniques of navigation!) under the heading of R. E. Hanging terrestrial hats on celestial pegs, as it were.

Thirdly, we have the data of R. E. more or less completely abandoned and replaced by the data of morality. At its best, this approach may aspire to the evaluation of rival ethical systems. At its worst it degenerates into the far from moral imperative: 'knock a bit of moral teaching into 4G!'

I reckon that none of these three approaches is R. E. itself and I make no apology for stating bluntly that the first — fundamentalism — should never be taught for the very good reason that it is false and can be shown to be false. It serves only to give the whole of R. E. a bad name. 'World Faiths' evades the central religious question of the existence of God by talking about the possible existence of gods: good anthropology but not very good theology and therefore not really the substance of R. E.

The provision of an ethics course (however informal or however well structured) is the practical result of the unspoken assumption that religion is outdated — an irrelevant anachronism. As Rudolf Bultmann used to say: 'You can't believe that sort of thing in an age of electric light and the wireless'.

Now I believe that the basic questions of religion are still worth pondering and I have found an awakening interest on the pupils' part when these questions are presented honestly in straightforward language and discussed openly without the pressure of dogmatism from wherever it may come.

What are these questions? They are those of endless fascination: 'Is there a God?' 'Do miracles happen?' 'Is there a life after death?' 'Has science disproved religion' 'Why do people suffer?' Here is scope for an interesting year's work with 15+ pupils. I make no final conclusions and that is why we have called the book *Thinking About Religion*.

Peter Mullen

Contents

1 Is There A God?

I

Do you believe in God? It might be interesting to do a quick count in your class and see how many people do believe and how many do not. Up until about two hundred years ago the question would have seemed stupid to most people. God's existence used to be taken for granted — even by those who didn't attend church every week.

By 1770 the first part of the scientific revolution was complete. Galileo had looked long and deep into outer space through his telescope. Copernicus had let it be known that the world wasn't flat after all as everyone had supposed — men had even sailed around the earth and proved it. Kepler's laws of motion were well known in scientific quarters. And Newton's theories about gravitation were universally accepted.

There were one or two thinkers around like David Hume and Voltaire who questioned the existence of God. Some of their writings are mentioned at the end of this book. But most ordinary people still accepted the Bible as truth 'word for word' and they continued to believe that all the people living on the earth were under the care of the almighty God.

Now in the late twentieth century we've had a lot more scientific instruction about the universe. We probe into deep space with our radio telescope and discover strange things with even stranger names, black holes and white dwarfs. Physicists observe the workings of that micro cosmos (little universe) of the atom and invent strange titles for what they find there: electrons, protons, neutrons and the lovable quark.

So you might think that with all this new knowledge we don't need God as an explanation for the existence of the universe any longer. Science can explain everything — or nearly everything anyhow. But astonishingly the public opinion polls devised by market research people show that a majority of the population still believe in God. At the same time it turns out to be true that not so many people say their prayers or believe the miracle stories in the Bible. And the churches are almost empty. Many of them have had to be closed down and some turned into warehouses or bingo halls.

So why do so many people still believe in God? And what's the 'cash value' of their belief since they admit to not saying prayers and they don't believe any longer in miraculous events? One answer is that people are superstitious. They are encouraged by the workings of their intellect to say, 'All right: it seems more reasonable to believe in science than it does to believe in all that old-fashioned stuff about God. I therefore stop believing in him as from now'. But then a little doubt creeps in and they say, 'Oh well, God *most likely* doesn't exist, but I'll say I believe in him *just in case*. After all, what difference does it make?'

And in many cases that's all there is to it. Men and women who live in large cities and own television sets, pocket calculators and many other scientific marvels no longer behave as if God exists. He makes no difference to their lives. He isn't needed to explain anything. But people keep on believing, or at least saying they believe, just in case. And the 'just in case' means: 'It's barely possible that God exists, but if he does I might meet him after death — and then what?' Fear of hell? Of the 'bare possibility' of hell? I don't know. But someone once called twentieth-century man's claim to believe in God a form of fire insurance! And if you have a good look around you'll find that even scientifically minded people harbour the most odd superstitions.

Exercises
(1) Someone once said of God, 'I have no need of that hypothesis'. Why do you think so many people still claim to believe in God in our age of science?
(2) Why are even the most intelligent people superstitious at times?
(3) Are you one of the people who takes out 'fire insurance'? Is it worth the premium? And what's the chance of this policy maturing?

II

So far we've looked very generally at how people feel about the idea of God. Science and commonsense enquiry start by questioning and arguing in a reasonable way. It's possible to approach the idea of God like this. In fact certain traditional arguments have been put forward in favour of God's existence. Let's have a look at some of them.

The Ontological Argument

This simply means the argument from being. It was first put forward by a man called Anselm who lived between 1033 and 1109. Perhaps it should be made clear from the start that Anselm was already a Christian when he began to frame his ontological argument. He wasn't converted to Christianity or to belief in God by the argument. In fact in a famous sentence he said, 'I do not seek to understand that I may believe, but because I already believe I wish to understand'.

Anselm began by saying what he meant by the word 'God'. That's one method of what we call 'defining' or 'definition'. And he said that the word

'God' stands for *a being than which nothing greater can be imagined*. So, in a way, Anselm had really said, 'It is impossible *not* to believe in God because everyone must have some idea of the greatest being'. Sometimes when philosophers talk about this argument they say they are discussing the 'necessary existence' of God. For Anselm the ontological argument does not rely on anything observed in the world. It is a purely logical argument — in the head, like mental arithmetic. And it can be denied only by the arguer contradicting himself. Therefore it must be true — or so he thought.

But what if we say, 'Fair enough I can think of a being greater than which cannot be imagined but that doesn't mean such a being exists in reality'. Anselm had quoted from an Old Testament Psalm: 'The fool has said in his heart, "There is no God" '. A scholar called Gaunilo put forward our 'Fair enough . . .' argument in a book which he called *On Behalf of the Fool!*

Gaunilo went on to say that he could imagine the most perfect island, a paradise on earth. But it didn't follow from this that such an island actually existed on the earth. And so with the idea of a perfect being, a being greater than which cannot be imagined. It's easy to see that such a being exists *in the imagination,* but that doesn't mean he or it or whatever exists *in fact.*

Anselm answered Gaunilo by saying that he was absolutely right in his argument about the perfect island but God was a special case. In fact the unique case. And that's because in the case of God we're considering not just the most perfect thing of its kind — like a perfect island (one among many islands), a perfect horse (one among many horses) or a perfect lunch (one among many lunches). But we're considering the most perfect of any and all kinds. That there must be such a perfection seemed self-evident to Anselm. And that perfection, that greatest and most perfect being, he called God.

Do you agree with Anselm or with the fool? Many thinkers have rejected Anselm's argument as mistaken or simply too far-fetched. But it's interesting to notice that the ontological argument has fascinated philosophers and theologians since the Middle Ages down to the present day.

A Frenchman called Descartes (1596-1650) gave his attention to the argument and came out firmly in support. He was a mathematician — indeed the one who thought up that formula for solving quadratic equations. So in more ways than one he was no fool! That doesn't mean he was right, of course, in everything he said. But the following is the gist of his approach.

Descartes said he could imagine in his mind a triangle which had never existed — one which had never been drawn. So, he claimed, it didn't exist. But the odd thing about this non-existing triangle was that in all other ways it was exactly like any other triangle which did exist. For example, it had three sides and three angles. Its area could be calculated by multiplying half the base by the perpendicular height. And its internal angles added up to $180°$. So Descartes argued that just as having three sides and three angles is necessary to the idea of a triangle, existence is necessary to the idea of a perfect being: God.

Perhaps you find this argument convincing? Or maybe you think it's just as mistaken whether stated by Anselm or as revised by Descartes? Philosophers still consider it, and in *The Many Faced Argument* listed at the end of this book you'll find another volume completely devoted to a discussion of the ontological argument. That book was written by men who earn their living by teaching and writing about philosophy and theology in our universities. And it was published in 1968 so you can see Anselm's old argument is still a live issue. So there's plenty of room for discussion. Here there's only space to mention two further criticisms of the ontological argument. One is direct and was written in the eighteenth century. The other is indirect and belongs to our own time.

Immanuel Kant lived from 1724 until 1804. He thought Descartes' version of the argument was false and so he set about disproving it. Changing Descartes' triangles to dollars, Kant argued that real dollars and imaginary dollars were quite different things. In effect what he said was, 'You just try adding imaginary dollars to real dollars in your bank account and see where that gets you with your budget — not to mention the bank manager!'

And then he added, more subtly, that the idea of a thing existing adds nothing to the simple original idea of it. By this he meant that if I tell you that the school is new and large and has a swimming-bath inside, then I certainly tell you something. But if I add to the information that the school which is new and large and has a swimming-bath that it also exists, then I'm not really giving you any information at all. In short, existence unlike newness, largeness and having a swimming-bath isn't a characteristic (philosophers sometimes say 'a quality') of a thing at all. To think of something as existing adds nothing to your original thought of the thing. For when you think of it (whatever 'it' is) it exists in your thoughts. If you think of it existing *in fact,* it still only exists *in fact in your thoughts.*

The second and indirect argument might interest you if you like language and grammar. You know that a sentence can be divided into two parts and that these can be named, as follows:

Subject	*Predicate*
The boy	stood on the burning deck

Well an English philospher G. E. Moore (1873-1958) wrote, '... existence is not a predicate'. And this is what he meant. Suppose I tell you that some tame tigers do not growl, then we can analyse the sentence into subject and predicate like this:

Subject	*Predicate*
Some tame tigers	do not growl

Now the predicate 'do not growl' tells me something about the subject 'Some tame tigers'. But suppose I try to treat 'exist' as a predicate? Let's look and see what happens then:

Subject	*Predicate*
Some tame tigers	do not exist

Obviously this is nonsense. For I'm asserting the existence of something
— 'Some tame tigers' — and then I'm denying that assertion — 'do not exist'.
So the whole sentence 'Some tame tigers do not exist' is nonsense because
it is contradictory. That means it says something and then unsays it. It is
therefore uninformative.

Now simply to go on from there and reverse the meaning of that
sentence does us no good either. For if 'Some tame tigers *do not* exist'
is to say something and then to unsay it, if it is a contradiction and therefore
uninformative, then its opposite 'Some tame tigers *do* exist' is merely to
say something and then to say it again. It is similarly uninformative. In
other words you can't conjure *real* tame tigers into existence simply by
saying that they exist. That's what G. E. Moore meant when he said,'. . .
existence is not a predicate.'

Summary
The ontological argument is concerned with logic and pure reason. That
means it tries to demonstrate the existence of God by an examination of
words and ideas alone. It tries to say that the existence of God is self-
evident or necessary. It has been supported by Anselm and Descartes. The
only way to refute the ontological argument is by trying to show that it is
not self-evident and that it is contradictory. Gaunilo and Kant thought
they had refuted it. Some arguments in modern philosophy, for example
by G. E. Moore, seem to indicate the conclusion that it is contradictory
although the debate still continues.

Exercises and Things to do
*(1) Is the idea of 'God' different from the idea of an 'island' not just in
    content but in some other absolute sense as Anselm suggested?*
(2) Arrange a debate between Anselm and Gaunilo.
*(3) Does Descartes' version of the ontological argument add any new
    insight to the argument as put forward by Anselm?*
(4) Does it make sense to talk about 'necessary existence'?
(5) What is meant by saying that existence is not a predicate?

The Cosmological Argument

This argument is more down to earth than the previous one. It doesn't
proceed from logic or what Kant called 'pure reason' but actually looks at
the world and tries to prove that the very fact of the world's existence
demands the existence of God. In other words, that the world, as it exists
and as we perceive it, needs the action of God in order to account for its
existence.

The cosmological argument (cosmos = world) can be put as follows.

Everything that there is came from something else. I came from my
parents. They from theirs and so on right back through evolution to

the first signs of life on the planet. Earth itself came from off the
sun. The sun is a star among many stars. These came from atoms of helium
The helium was formed through the rapid movement of hydrogen atoms
God made the hydrogen atoms.

It doesn't matter which particular theory of creation's history you take.
The cosmological argument claims to be valid for all such theories. Do you
think the world began with Adam and Eve? Very well, who made them?
Did it all start off quite differently with a few atoms of cosmic dust? So
where did the cosmic dust come from? Was the origin of the universe a big
bang? Then who was responsibile for the bang?

The cosmological argument is about what happened in the first place.
Those who support it (they include the great theologian and saint, Thomas
Aquinas: 1225-1274) will not allow that history just stretches back into
time forever. They don't believe in infinite series when it comes to things.
It's all right for numbers. You can, at least in theory, go on counting forever.
But objects we can touch and see must have had a beginning. And, so it is
argued, if a beginning then a creator. And that creator they call 'God'.

The first objection to this argument is simply put: 'Why need there ever
have been a beginning? I see no compelling reason to think that things
haven't always existed in some shape or form'.

Sometimes the reply to this might be: 'Well, everything you see in the
world had a beginning at one time or another, so it's reasonable to assume
that the world itself had a beginning. And if a beginning, then somebody
must have begun it'.

The philosopher Bertrand Russell (1872-1970) questioned this. He said,
'Because all the parts of the whole had a beginning is not sufficient reason
to believe that the whole itself had a beginning'. In other words, to ask,
'Where did shoes come from' or even 'Where did the dinosaurs come from'
are questions different in type from the question 'Where did *it all* come from?'

Another objection to the cosmological argument asks quite abruptly
'Who made God?' And this isn't as silly or as childish as it sounds. For if
you're not satisfied with cosmic dust or hydrogen atoms as the first thing
in the universe, then why be satisfied with God as the first cause either?

If the reply is, 'Ah, well you see, all those other things depend on God
for their existence, but God is different from them in that he made them.
He is eternal'. Then someone might answer: 'How do you know?' Two
replies might possibly follow:
(1) 'I know God is eternal because he is the one who made all that there
     is. He must be the First Cause. He must be eternal.'
To this the answer is simple: 'But that God made all that there is, is precisely
what is at question. So you're just arguing in a circle.'
(2) 'God is different. He is defined as the First Cause of the universe.
     That's what the word "God" means.'
The answer to this brings us back to familiar territory: 'But why should I
accept your definition of what "God" means? And how do you know that
your definition of God, in your own mind and in words, corresponds with

any such *real* being? This is just the ontological argument you're giving me all over again! For unless you can prove *on other grounds* that God exists, there's no reason for me to accept your definition of him.'

Summary
The cosmological argument seeks to demonstrate the existence of God from the fact of the existence of the universe: 'Someone *must* have made it'. It is based on a strong dislike of an infinite series of events (sometimes called 'an infinite regress'). But it may be objected that, while each individual thing in creation was created or formed out of something which came before it, there's no sufficient reason to suppose that the whole universe must have had a beginning. Furthermore, simply to bring in the idea of God as a creator, or first term in the series, doesn't make any useful contribution to the argument since the question can always be asked, 'Who made God?' If the reply is that no one made God for he is, by definition, the eternal creator, then this has no logical power to persuade, for there is no reason why anyone should accept that particular definition. The attempt to define God into existence is merely a version of the ontological argument whose defects are well known.

Exercises and Things to Do
(1) Explain what is meant by an infinite regress. Why does it seem all right to have an infinite regress of numbers but not of events?
(2) Must there have been a first cause?
(3) How does the cosmological argument, according to one theory, turn out to depend upon the ontological proof of God's existence?
(4) Which argument do you find more plausible, the ontological or the cosmological? Why?

The Teleological Argument

'Teleological' is a big word which comes from a Greek word meaning 'purpose'. And the teleological argument for the existence of God starts out by looking at the world and finding purpose in it. So if there is purpose or design in the world, there must be a purposeful mind or a designer behind it. This designer the argument calls 'God'.

One of the most famous defenders of this argument was an eighteenth century archdeacon who lived at roughly the same time as Immanuel Kant. His name was William Paley (1743-1805) and his version of the teleological argument is based on an example he gave of a man finding a watch on the sands. Suppose he'd never seen a watch before? He would still conclude from the intricate mechanism that it had been made for some purpose — that behind it was an intelligent mind.

So Mr Paley says that if we look at the world we will see so much evidence of design and purpose in it that we shall be bound to conclude 'The world has a maker'.

There is some power in this argument. Don't we see that night follows day? That the seasons of the year return in due course and in proper order? Our bodies are ordered in a suitable way to the tasks we need to perform in order to live? Surely this is proof enough of order and design and therefore a designer who is none other than God!

We should not be surprised (by now!) to discover that there are objections even to this persuasive argument. First, there's the criticism arising from evolutionary theories which came to light last century. According to these the world order wasn't created for the benefit of mankind but men and women have developed into the creatures that they now are as a result of the way the world is. In other words, we shouldn't say, 'How convenient these arms are for swinging on trees' but 'We've developed arms because in our search for food and in our attempts to escape from enemies we have needed to swing on trees'. This is another way of saying that such order as we might think we see in the world is only the end-product of our (and the other animals') struggle for survival. Order wasn't specially created for us. Rather the boot is on the other foot. We have, over a long period of time, managed to adjust to the world as it is in the raw. If we hadn't done so, we wouldn't have survived and there's an end of it.

We can add to this and say that rather than order being something which exists in the world it is merely a concept in our own minds. Something which we invent — like arithmetic — in order to deal with the vast, confusing chaos that we're faced with every day. In this sense, order is something like the laws of cricket or the rules of tennis. Something we put on to the world to make sense of it, in much the same way as those baffling events at Lords can only be explained by looking into the (man-made) rules of the game.

Before the last century and the rise of evolutionary theories, the argument from design was very popular. You see, people accepted the Genesis account of creation where everything in all the world was made and ordered for the use and the sake of the crowning glory of God's work — mankind. Charles Darwin (1809-1882) showed that the actual history of the world was the other way about. That, far from being the lucky inheritor of a primeval order, man himself, by his own efforts has struggled against chaos and danger to the, even now, precarious security he enjoys. Rather than enjoy order, we have managed to adapt to disorder. But there is another objection to the teleological argument which concentrates its attack on what might be called 'bad design'.

Bad Design — The Problem of Evil
Even if we took no notice of the evolutionary theories and their criticism of the teleological argument, there is another objection so strong that it has prevented many people from accepting the idea of God. And this objection is based on the existence of evil in the world. Perhaps evil seems to point to bad design.

Here's a list of the kinds of things meant by evil in the world:

(1) The death of young children.
(2) Disease.
(3) Disasters like earthquakes and floods.
(4) Pain and suffering.
(5) Wars.

Surely these are evidence enough that the world is badly designed and organized? That it's a chaos and a mess? Whatever God (if he exists) is like, he is most frequently said to be a good God. In that case, why evil? The Scottish philosopher David Hume (1711-1776) wrote a great deal about this problem notably in *Dialogues,* chapters 10 and 11; further references to his works are at the back of this book. The outline of the argument is as follows.

It is said that God is all-powerful and completely good. But we observe as a matter of fact the presence of evil in the world. If God would like to put an end to evil but cannot, then he is not all-powerful. If he can but will not, then he is not all good. If he is all-powerful and all good, then where does evil come from? A mighty big problem!

The Freewill Defence

One line of defence open to the believer challenged by David Hume's criticism is based on the idea that God has given men and women freewill. This is to say that if only human beings would choose good (God's will) and not choose the bad then evil would be diminished. For instance, if men would love their neighbours and turn the other cheek as it says in the Bible, there would be no wars and murders. So there would be an end to the evil they bring.

In the same way, if people would share the earth's goods there would be no need for half of mankind to go undernourished. Instead man is greedy and grabs the lion's share for himself while weaker members of the human race in poorer countries starve to death.

So the freewill defence says that the answer to the problem of evil is to be found in doing the will of God.

The trouble with this defence is that it doesn't seem to cover all cases. For example, by being loving and kind we might learn to put an end to wars. But war is only one contributing factor to the sum of human misery. What about earthquakes and floods? Children killed by lightning? Virulent plagues and diseases? Surely these evils in the natural order cannot be put down to human sinfulness?

The Best of All Possible Worlds

Gottfried Leibnitz (1646-1716) argued that although there is undoubtedly evil in the world, this is unavoidable. Some evils, he thought, exist so that we may enjoy greater good later on. You might be able to think of a few examples here. For instance, there's the case of the athlete suffering pain during training so that at some time in the future he may experience the greater good of taking part in (and perhaps winning) the big race. So it is argued some evil is necessary and that the world we have, though not ideal, is the best of all possible worlds.

Whatever Leibnitz and others say about the best of all possible worlds, their explanation of the purpose of evil seems to many people an attack on the idea of God as an all-powerful God. We want to ask, 'What d'you say, he's all-powerful and *this* is the best he can do?' We think perhaps that a better world than this one shouldn't be beyond the ability of an almighty creator God.

Will It All Work Out in Heaven?
Some modern thinkers, including John Hick (b. 1922) who wrote a book called *Evil and the God of Love,* say that God's purposes stretch beyond this life and that the purpose of evil will be made clear when we're in heaven. Can you believe that? I'm not sure. And that's because Professor Hick's theory replaces *one* unknown with *two.* Added to the question of whether, in the face of all the evil in the world, God exists comes the other vexed question: 'Is there a life after death?' John Hick may be right, of course, but the point seems to be that people want pointers on how best to live *this life* drawn *from* this life. And to ask them to wait in faith for a life to come (a life the reality of which has not been proved) for an explanation of evil is in the end to ask too much.

Summary
Another argument for the existence of God is the argument from design or the teleological argument. This works from the fact that we observe order in the universe to the conclusion that the universe itself is the creation of a supernatural mind. This mind is called God. The theory of evolution has cast doubts on the whole idea of order in the world, saying instead that such order as appears is not for the special benefit of man but is merely the natural scheme in which man has been forced to adapt in order to survive.

One explanation for disorder or evil in the world is that it is all man's fault. If we were kind and loving toward one another there would not be wars and murders. But this doesn't seem to account for natural disasters.

The explanation that this is the best of all possible worlds appears to limit the power of the creator. And the notion that all will be explained after death seems only to postpone rather than solve the problem.

Exercises and Things to Do
(1) Is there design in the world or is what we see of the natural order 'just the way it happens to be?'
(2) 'Even if the existence of order in the universe were to count as proof of the existence of a designer there is no reason to suppose this designer is a God of love. Perhaps the universe was made by a very precise machine.' Talk about this in class.
(3) How did David Hume use the problem of evil as an attack on the belief that there is a God?
(4) Is this the best of all possible worlds?

(5) *What do you think about Mr Hick's point that we can't know all there is to know about this life while we're still living it?*

The Argument from Religious Experience

One approach to the problem of whether there is a God or not goes something like this: 'Well I'm not troubled by all your silly arguments. They're just logic chopping and mere words. I *know* God exists because I've experienced him. And that's an end of the matter!' The speaker might go on to relate an experience which he's had — an experience he found moving, uplifting or comforting. Sometimes people even claim to have seen a vision of God, of Jesus Christ or of the Blessed Virgin Mary. What then are we to make of the argument from religious experience?

We should stress that usually these experiences are extremely powerful and therefore they possess great power to convince. Just remember how St Paul's vision of Christ on the road to Damascus so changed his mind that he became, instantly, perhaps the most enthusiastic Christian the world has ever seen. What d'you think Paul would say if you suggested he'd been mistaken — all he'd seen was an illusion?

And yet this is the first move in the attempt to refute the argument from religious experience. How do we know that such experiences, however intense, are based firmly in reality and not just on a piece of undigested cheese? It seems very rude to belittle people's most meaningful experiences in this way. But the question must be faced for it will be asked by every enquiring philosopher. Besides, to suggest that these strange and moving experiences are not caused by God but by some natural force is not to belittle the experiences themselves. Only to question their cause. A psychologist called Sigmund Freud (1856-1939) said that all such experiences were connected to a widespread and fairly mild form of mental illness which he called neurosis. In short he argued that the conclusions drawn from religious experiences, so called, were simply so much wishful thinking. It must be admitted it is difficult to prove that all or even any such feelings originate in heaven. The problem for the unbeliever though is to account for their power to persuade, to convince and to change people's whole way of life. You've all heard stories of the thief and the drunkard who 'saw the light' and altered his ways from that day onwards.

One question arises. If God wants all men to know of his existence, why doesn't he reveal himself more clearly and to all people instead of just to a few? Like the problem of evil, it's said of this question that we can't hope to plumb the depths of God's mind in this life. But if the fact of unusual experiences in the lives of a minority is allowed to count as evidence for the existence of God, shouldn't the lack of such experiences in the lives of the majority count as evidence against?

Whatever we make of religious experience it is by itself no proof of God's existence.

Summary

Some people claim to know that God exists because they say they have experienced him directly. It is impossible to tell whether what is called 'religious experience' really is what it says or whether it is something else — an illusion perhaps. Why doesn't God, if he exists, give religious experiences to everyone? The argument is inconclusive.

Exercise and Things to Do
(1) Have you ever had a religious experience? What was it like?
(2) How can we tell that religious experiences are what they seem to be and not simply illusions or the result of indigestion?
(3) If God exists, why doesn't he make his existence plain?

III

Another Approach I Wonder?

Let's start by assuming that all the arguments on the preceding pages are false. What does that prove? Not that there is no God. Only that we can't demonstrate his existence by arguments. So where can we begin? Let's have another look at our idea of defining God. All the above arguments have a very clear idea of what 'God' means. So that they almost assume at the beginning the reality of what they're out to prove.

Now what is the process of definition about anyway? Well, suppose I define a pencil case as 'a receptacle for storing pencils, usually quite small, generally portable'. Apart from commenting on the style and decoration of individual pencil cases, I've said just about all there is to be said about the essence of what we mean by 'a pencil case'. I've surrounded it and trapped it in words. I've defined it. I've said exactly what it is. Now that's all very well with pencil cases — and even here some people would disagree saying I haven't defined it properly or accurately enough. But what if I move away from pencils and ink bottles and desks and rulers? What if I try to define what we mean by 'a game' or 'a person'? To cut a long story short it becomes exceedingly difficult if not impossible.

And yet I've seen all these things, had direct experience of them. In some cases I've talked to them and touched them. Still the problem of definition won't go away. So it's hardly surprising when we come to consider the idea of God that definition, let alone proof, escapes us completely. For if God is what believers say he is — a supernatural being who is all-powerful and all-knowing and who made everything there is — it's hardly surprising that we can't ensnare him in our definitions and make him the plaything of our arguments.

I know that this approach could sound like yet another argument for the existence of God — an argument more dishonest than all the others put together. It might be called 'the argument from obscurity'! But I believe there's more to it than that, though I'd like to say that what there is in the 'more to it' is rather in the nature of hints than arguments.

The Evidence From Science

Some people have got the idea into their heads that science explains everything. And that as 'scientific progress', as it is sometimes called, goes on, the world is being rendered more easily understood. Things are getting simpler. But this is a caricature of science. Those who maintain it have heads that are too big and not enough body! For the reverse is true. Take the following two examples.

Primitive science looked up into the sky and saw the sun, the moon and the stars. These were thought to be small bodies but quite important ones — important that is for us down here on the flat earth. The point being that early science believed the whole universe existed just for the sake of earthlings.

Later science discovered that we on this planet are but one among a company encircling the sun. We're no longer the centre of the universe. It's bigger than we thought.

Modern science peers far into space and sees that, in size terms anyway, our solar system — even the galaxy itself — is a tiny speck on the interstellar map. And we admit into our vocabulary terms such as 'pulsars', 'quasars', 'black holes', 'naked singularities', 'curved space' and 'the expanding universe'. (Expanding into what for goodness sake?)

In short it hasn't become simpler but infinitely more complicated and vastly more wonderful. Much more amazing than the view of the world possessed in ancient times. What are we going to discover next I wonder?

And then let's look 'downwards and inwards' instead of 'upwards and outwards'. Where the ancients and the Renaissance scientists saw only 'specks' and 'molecules' and 'atoms' about which they formulated rigid laws, present-day scientists look within the atom at individual electrons. And beyond these at 'neutrinos' and 'quarks', and at a particle they call 'charm'. And, what's this I hear? In 1927 the physicist Werner Heisenberg found out that it is impossible to measure the position and speed of sub-atomic particles with any real precision. And so quantum mechanics must include an 'uncertainty principle'! More than that, sometimes these sub-atomic particles behave as if they're particles while on other occasions they behave like waves. So that scientists aren't at all sure of the nature of matter itself.

These two examples make me look at the universe and wonder. And basically what I wonder is this: 'If our present state of knowledge couldn't possibly have been imagined a hundred years ago, what might things appear like in another hundred years? A thousand? A hundred thousand? A million? Doesn't the history of science show us that the universe is wonderful beyond our wildest science fiction?'

And so the more our knowledge increases the more I think we've cause to wonder. When we wonder like this we are less likely to make hasty and dogmatic statements such as 'there *can't be* a God' or as a theologian called Rudolf Bultmann (b. 1884) once wrote of miracle stories, 'You can't believe that sort of thing in an age of electric light and the wireless' I would have thought that the 'miracles' of electric light and the wireless might make anything seem possible!

And then when we turn to look at the human mind in the present-day study of psychology, we see all sorts of chemical reactions at work and we see the mind affecting the body (and vice versa) in ways that would never have been believed during the nineteenth century. So it appears that matter is becoming more incorporeal (bodyless or spiritual) while mind is becoming more solid (physical and chemical). Whoever would have thought such things?

The Evidence from Art
By art I mean all creative human actions — and that often includes science especially in the moment of invention. But I'm thinking particularly of music, literature and painting. How is it that great works of art seem to come to us from another realm entirely? How is it that they seem so often to uplift us to that realm? How is it that creative artists speak so often of 'inspiration' — that the work was not their own but something (someone?) worked through them?

The Evidence from Life in General
Perhaps this is the best evidence of all that there might, despite all our misgivings, be something to the idea of God more than just an academic talking point. I'm thinking of those people who give up their whole lives in service of others because they believe that's what God wants them to do. Then there are those who suffer immense pain at the hands of their enemies and yet have the strength to forgive. You might like to look at the story of Dietrich Bonhoeffer in his own book *Letters and Papers from Prison*. Or perhaps St Matthew's gospel!

I'm not saying that any of these points proves the existence of God. Proof in any subject is an extremely difficult business. Have a look at Descartes', Berkeley's and Bertrand Russell's various attempts to prove that there is a world at all! Or just try and prove to everyone's satisfaction that your best friend really exists. This isn't to say that argument and trying to prove or disprove the existence of God is all a waste of time. Far from it. It will sharpen your wits if nothing else. But looking at science, art and the world in general with as few prejudices as possible might stir up a few new thoughts in your minds. It makes me wonder. It makes me wonder whether God might not turn out to be there after all. Does it make you wonder? Are you sure?

Exercise and Things to Do
(1) Does the fact that science is showing the world to be more complicated than we ever imagined it make you think it more or less likely that there is a God?

(2) Try to prove something. Anything that's not to do with mathematics.

(3) Are artists and musicians talking nonsense when they talk about inspiration?

2 Heaven and Hell

In the last century some churchmen brought out a book called *Essays and Reviews*. It was an attempt to try and square the biblical account of the world and man's place in it with the new discoveries in science — especially the doctrine of evolution. *Essays and Reviews* appeared in 1860, just one year after Charles Darwin's famous book *The Origin of Species*.

Perhaps the task was altogether too difficult. Maybe the writers were too close to the events they were discussing to do justice to both sides: to science and to religion. But they were men of goodwill honestly trying to make sense of the Christian faith in the light of the new knowledge. So it's a pity that they were so misunderstood and persecuted by the church at large. The authors were brought to trial in the ecclesiastical courts after 137,000 lay people and 11,000 clergy had signed a petition against their work. Here the case went against them and they were deprived of their official positions in the church for a year. But two of them Williams and Wilson, appealed to the Privy Council against their conviction. And the decision of the church courts was reversed. One of the chapters in *Essays and Reviews* denied the existence of an everlasting hell to which sinners go after death. And that was what particularly upset the 'proper' people who made up the Church of England in 1860. They thought to themselves: 'We go to church every week and say our prayers. If God is going to allow sinners [by which they meant non-churchgoers] to go to heaven, then what's been the point of all our devotion to private prayer and public worship? It's not fair!'

A wit, writing at the time, satirized their hypocrisy. Of the Privy Council's decision to acquit Williams and Wilson he wrote: 'The Lord Chancellor dismissed hell with costs and took away from orthodox members of the Church of England their last hope of everlasting damnation'. It's a pity but it does look sometimes as if the so called 'righteous' people (the goodies) can only expect to enjoy their reward properly if the 'unrighteous' people (the baddies) are seen to get their just deserts.

Well, what can we make of the ideas of heaven and hell in our own so called 'enlightened times'? Perhaps we should have a look at how these concepts arose in the first place and the powerful influence they have exercised over people's minds down the years. Then we might be in a better position to see if they retain any value for us or if they should be thrown on the rubbish tip of outmoded ideas and theories.

Universal Ideas

Whether or not there is an actual heaven and a real hell we'll leave for a little speculation later on. One thing we can't get away from is that nearly all civilizations have entertained the idea of heaven and hell and so it would be unreasonable and unscientific to ignore that fact. It's not the purpose of this book to describe in detail exactly what images of the afterlife were (and still are) held by folk the world over. This has been done many times and recently very clearly and pictorially in a book called *Visions of Heaven and Hell* by Richard Cavendish. You can find further details about this and other useful books in the bibliography at the back.

But it seems to be true that most cultures and religions have taken up one of two opposing stories on the nature of the afterlife. There are those who say that the departed spirit will need a body with which to enjoy heaven (or to suffer hell!). Others claim that the life following physical death is a spiritual existence and doesn't depend on a body at all. Of the first opinion Richard Cavendish writes amusingly:

> The old belief that the dead lived on in their tombs persisted. Offerings of food and drink were brought to them and letters were posted to them. They were provided with furniture, utensils and equipment of all sorts, including lavatories.

He's talking about the ancient Egyptians and their practice of mummification known to every man, woman and child in this country if not thanks to the education system at least by courtesy of Boris Karloff, Peter Cushing and their horror films.

As a contrast with this highly physical idea of the afterlife stands the religion of the Buddha which makes the aim of each individual soul the escape from what has been called 'the tyranny of existence' into the Absolute or Nirvana. How we are to conceive of the Buddhists' Absolute isn't always clear. Certainly we're not to imagine it as having anything to do with earthly, bodily or physical existence. 'Blessed non-existence' or 'Incorporation into the unmoving totality' are phrases which suggest its nature — if we can make any sense of them. E. O. James comments:

> The Buddha himself claimed to have had a foretaste of it at the moment of his Enlightenment, and although he was not able to define Nirvana he realised that it was the end of the earthly struggle with pain and desire; complete emancipation from all the fetters and from the conceit of individuality.

Well, if the Buddha himself couldn't define his Absolute or Nirvana, perhaps we may be excused for maintaining a respectful silence.

Despite the widespread idea that whatever comes after death we can't do anything about it here — someone once wrote that we're 'On a board untrue with a twisted cue and elliptical billiard balls'.

The idea of what kind of life we might enjoy or suffer on the other side of the grave, depending on how we behave in this life, soon became an important consideration in Christian thought.

The Jews of the Old Testament period didn't at first attach much significance to what happens after death. They believed in a kind of misty underworld, Hades or Sheol as they called it. Here the spirits of the departed lived a shadowy existence until eventually they faded away altogether. But by the end of the Old Testament period quite different ideas were emerging.

The Jewish people began to speculate about heaven and hell. Matthew Black tells us:

> I Enoch [a book dating from the first century B.C.] develops the ideas of heavenly abodes for the righteous after death and of places where the wicken are held until the judgment and their punishment in Gehenna [hell]. The abode of the righteous is known as Paradise, a Persian word for a park or garden . . . The opposite of Paradise is Gehenna originally the vale of Hinnom south of Jerusalem at one time a place for burning the city's rubbish . . . but now a symbol for the place of horror and torture for the wicked.

These ideas obviously influenced the writers of the New Testament who have quite definite opinions about heaven and hell. Here are just a few examples:

> . . . whoever says, 'you fool!' shall be liable to the hell [Gehenna] of fire. (Matthew 5:13)
> Blessed are you when men revile and persecute you . . . Rejoice and be glad for your reward is great in heaven. (Matthew 5:11-12)
> Just as the weeds are gathered and burned with fire, so will it be at the close of the age. The Son of Man will send his angels, and they will gather out of his kingdom all causes of sin and all evildoers, and throw them into the furnace of fire. Then the righteous shall shine like the sun in the kingdom of their Father. (Matthew 13:40-43)
> And they shall go away into eternal punishment, but the righteous into eternal life. (Matthew 25:46)
> And he will send out his angels and gather the elect from the . . . ends of heaven. (Mark 13:27)
> The rich man also died and was buried; and in Hell being in torment he lifted up his eyes . . . (Luke 16:23)
> For the wages of sin is death, but the free gift of God is eternal life in Christ Jesus our Lord. (Romans 6:23)
> For the Lord himself will descend from heaven with a cry of command, with the archangel's call, and with the sound of the trumpet of God. And the dead in Christ will rise first; then we who are alive, who are left, shall be caught up together with them in the

clouds to meet the Lord in the air; and so we shall always be with the Lord. (I Thessalonians 4:16-17)

Then Death and Hades were thrown into the lake of fire. This is the second death, the lake of fire. And if anyone's name was not found written in the book of life, he was thrown into the lake of fire. (Revelation 20:14-15)

Then I saw a new heaven and a new earth . . . God will wipe away every tear from their eyes and death shall be no more (Revelation 21:1-4 (part))

It would be an over simplification to imagine that the New Testament contains one pure and absolutely consistent doctrine about heaven and hell. It doesn't. The New Testament was written by many different people over a period of perhaps a hundred years and in that length of time ideas are bound to change and develop. But a general picture begins to emerge. Those who have done what is right in this life — sometimes this means simply believing that Jesus is the Son of God — will, after death, share eternal bliss with God in heaven. Those who have done wrong — or not believed in Jesus — will go to hell or 'outer darkness' as it is sometimes called. A place of torment or simply out of God's presence and beyond his love and care.

Sometimes heaven is pictured as a feast or banquet to which God invites the faithful, while the unfaithful and the unjust remain outside never to enjoy the glory of God's presence and the eternal happiness which that presence brings. But however heaven and hell are visualized, there's no denying the fact that these two alternatives have exercised a fascinating power and influence over the minds of believers and non-believers alike for the whole two thousand years of the Christian era. In a discussion of the Christian faith we can no more leave them out than we could omit French Impressionism from nineteenth-century art or the Beatles from the popular music of our own time.

Two Problems

It seems to me that there are two distinct problems closely connected with the concepts of heaven and hell. First, have we any good reason to suppose that there is a life after death in *any* form? And secondly, isn't the picture of heaven and hell an immoral one and not worthy of a good God? To put this another way: would the loving creator of the world, the Father of Jesus Christ who was the friend of outcasts and sinners, allow even one of his creatures to spend a bare five minutes let alone eternity in the terrors and torture of hell? Let's have a look at the first problem to start with. Is it reasonable to suppose that there is a life after death?

An Invisible Soul?

When you look at your friends in the street or at yourself in the mirror are you seeing all there is to see of what we mean by the word person? Clearly not — in one very simple and straightforward way at least. That is you can't see someone's brain, unless you open up his head. You can't even see the heart, liver and kidneys without first performing surgery or taking an X-ray picture. But in principle all these parts of the human body are visible — open to investigation.

There is a belief which has persisted since the earliest times that men and women aren't just body stuff but that they are soul stuff as well. The body is regarded as the outward and visible part of a person while the soul is the same person's invisible and inward nature. Some have gone on from this to argue that the soul — the invisible bit — is what makes you *you* and me *me*. And so those who argue in this way say the soul is eternal. It lasts forever. The body decays at death but the soul never perishes.

They say that your soul is the *real* you and my soul is the *real* me. It's as if the body is merely a house, an outer shell, which the soul uses because it's convenient to do so but which can simply be discarded at death.

In favour of this point of view is the fact that we're all different — not just in looks but in personality. The existence in each of us of an invisible soul is what gives us our distinct personalities, or so it is argued. For how else could we all be different individuals? Flesh and blood, brains, hearts and lungs are simply physical tissues. They couldn't possibly account for our individual natures and moods, our quite separate preferences, prejudices and desires. These are generated by the indwelling immortal soul. Perhaps they depend upon the body for their expression but they don't have their origin and cause within the physical body itself.

More than this, our individual souls are what ensure that we're recognizable *today* as the same people we were *yesterday*. The body, as we all know, changes and grows old. It is the *soul* of Jack Smith which makes Jack as a man of forty-five still recognizable as a development of Jack as a lad of eighteen. How often we say, 'D'you know, I met so and so the other day. I haven't seen him for seven years and he hasn't changed one bit'. Of course we don't mean he doesn't look older or taller or perhaps a little fatter, a little thinner. When we talk about, say, Jack Smith in this way we mean the 'Jack Smithness' of Jack Smith has stayed the same. So it's argued, this continuity is guaranteed by his invisible soul.

Can you think of an argument against the existence of such things as souls as I have just described them? Let's list a few objections briefly.

(1) If we can't see the soul, then how do we know it's there at all? Doctors are able to look into every part of a person's body but they've never located an organ called 'the soul'.

(2) The idea of an immortal soul is just an outmoded belief, a primitive superstition. Modern science tells us that what we call 'thoughts', 'ideas' or 'the mind' are simply electrical changes in a physical organ called the brain. There's no need to bring in shadowy and doubtful concepts such as 'the soul'.

(3) Of course we're all different. But that's not the work of an invisible
and mysterious soul dwelling unobserved within us. It's explained
quite clearly again by modern science in terms of our inherited
characteristics and our very different experiences early in our lives.
And it's these that make you *you* and me *me* — not some spooky
invisible thing.

It's pretty obvious that those who accept these as valid objections to
the existence of the soul can easily go on to deny a life after death. They
may say: 'We *are* our bodies, including of course the brain. No doubt we
are very wonderful creatures, complex in structure and individuals all of
us. But that doesn't alter the fact that *all* we are depends upon certain
electro-chemical changes taking place inside our skulls. Once those changes
are halted through either serious disease or sudden extensive damage then
we're dead and that's an end of us.'

This is only a brief summary of the arguments for and against the
existence of the soul. They are very complicated arguments and much has
been written about them. Once again you'll find plenty of recommendations
for further reading at the end of this book. Meanwhile, you might like to
arrange a debate: 'Does the soul exist?'

An Appetite for Heaven

This is a different argument altogether, though perhaps it depends upon
the existence of the immortal soul in the first place. It goes like this:
human beings have certain appetites. Hunger and thirst for example. Now
the means for the satisfaction of these appetites certainly exists in the
objects food and drink. You could make a similar point about tiredness
and sleep. Since we desire eternal life in the same way as we desire food,
then eternal life must exist as the object by which that desire (or
appetite) is actually satisfied. Moreover, if there was no such thing as a
life after death, then we wouldn't have an appetite for it.

There are people who find this approach appealing — convincing even.
But several points can be made against it:
(1) It is based on a false premise (that is a false foundation). And the
false premise is simply the one which states that all men desire eternal
life. *All* men become hungry and thirsty from time to time but *not
all* men desire to live forever.
(2) Even if it were true and all people did desire to live forever, that is no
proof of eternal life. Food and drink are things which belong to this
life — objects of our daily experience. Eternal life (if there is such a
thing) doesn't belong to the world of our daily experience and so we
can't compare it with things which do (like food and drink).
(3) The fact that we wish or hope or desire anything is no guarantee that
we shall ever receive it. You could hope to be the first woman on
Mars but unless the space agency chooses you for the mission you'll

be out of luck. There might not even be such a mission in any case.

The Evidence of Grief

In an interesting article Donald Mackinnon has argued that the fact that we grieve when one of our family or our friends dies is itself a kind of evidence for an afterlife. Here's what he says:

> But what of proof? How does one prove, for instance, that the agony of a person suddenly, and as it seems to him irrationally, bereaved is not a bubble on the surface of things? How does one confer on grief itself the dignity of validity? The jargon is repulsive: but in the end perhaps just *this* is the real issue. I spoke of the bereavement as seeming irrational: I spoke of the protest. At such a moment a person may be simultaneously conscious of life as having form, direction, meaning. And yet as having no form, no direction, no meaning. The violence of the disturbance is due to the fact, not that meaning has never been found, but that suddenly it has been taken away — as if by a malignant practical joker. Some philosophers insist with good reason that such a phrase as 'the meaning of life' is empty of sense. But if they are altogether right, then the very anguish of spirit I have been describing is shown up as trivial and empty. And is this something we can allow? It is less a pinchbeck survival than the place of man in the world that is at issue. Almost we would beg the world that it does not treat our agonies as nothings.

You can see what MacKinnon is getting at in his sentence 'But if they are altogether right then the very anguish of spirit I have been describing is shown up as trivial and empty'. He's saying that the experience of grief when one of our friends dies is such a deep and disturbing experience that it convinces us that human beings count for something. It's as if he protests: 'Don't tell me there's no more to life than a few passing years then the grave when I have experiences as strong as this!'

This is a powerful point. But what we must ask ourselves is whether it's a powerful point as an argument or simply in its ability to generate emotion. MacKinnon is right to claim that we're offended when we're told that even our deepest feelings count for nothing in the end — that they're trivial. But perhaps we need to get used to being offended and come to see our proper place in the universe and stop drawing exaggerated and romantic pictures of ourselves.

Let me try and explain this in a little more detail. In the past, man has pictured his role in the universe as a very great one. Here he stands as the discoverer of all secrets; a creature made in the very likeness of God; a noble participant in the eternal battle between the forces of light and the forces of darkness. This is the view of man we get from the Bible and from much non-biblical literature as well. Now suppose, after thousands of years of having this idea stamped all over his religion, his art and his music, man is suddenly told that as a matter of fact it isn't like this at all. And what is it like?

Well, men and women are highly evolved creatures but they're not different in kind from the rest of the animals. The difference is merely one of degree. Moreover, human beings live on a tiny planet which revolves around one of many billions of billions of ordinary average stars. The universe existed for billions of years before man and it will continue to exist for billions of years after he has (like many other animals) become extinct. Man should therefore discard all grandiose beliefs about his 'ultimate significance' for these are delusions. Instead he should cultivate a little decency in the way he lives his very ordinary life. In short man is *not* God. Man is *man*.

That's basically the argument against Donald MacKinnon's view. If it's a valid objection we ought to accept it of course. This will mean drastically scaling down our exalted picture of ourselves. It will mean that great chunks of pride will have to be swallowed. But better to swallow our pride than to persist in believing what is not true. Better to be upset and offended than to cherish a delusion as if it were an incontrovertible fact.

Pascal's Wager

The idea of this book is to encourage you to ponder these unknown things yourselves, but before summing up this part of the chapter, it's worth mentioning Blaise Pascal (1623-1662) and his unusual approach to the problem of life after death. Pascal wrote: 'The heart has its reasons of which reason knows not'. And he believed that from a logical point of view it is best in any case to accept the doctrine of life after death. The point of his famous wager, or bet, is quite simply stated: I will stake everything on the belief that there is a life after death. If I'm right, then that's all to the good because I shall have lived my life conscious of its reference to eternity and I shall awake after death to enjoy eternal bliss. If I'm wrong it doesn't matter, because if I'm not to live on after death, then I'll never know that I was wrong.

The Story So Far

We've looked at several arguments for and against the reality of an afterlife. The only certainty we've come across is that neither the believer nor the unbeliever can completely prove his case to the other's satisfaction. We've not yet raised the idea of God as responsible for us before and after our death. Here we shall begin to examine the biblical notion of eternal life where everything depends upon God. And we'll try to make some sense out of the words 'Heaven' and 'Hell'.

Life After Death — Reward and Punishment

Of course we haven't proved beyond reasonable doubt that God exists (see the last chapter). So is it really fair to proceed on the assumption that he does and then try to base our ideas on that unproved assumption? Aren't we going to end up with an odd sort of simultaneous equation, one with *two* unknown quantities 'God' *and* 'Life after death' — moreover a simultaneous equation of that particularly nasty sort: an unsolvable one?

Perhaps this will be our judgement of the matter in the end. But accepting for a minute that, while we can't prove that God exists, we can't disprove his existence either, we might suspend the dispute for a little while and see whether or not the acceptance of the existence of God throws any light on our other problem — life after death. After all, this is a good scientific procedure: think up a hypothesis and then try to test it.

So, for argument's sake, let's assume that there is a God and that the goal of human life is eventual eternal life with him after death. Now if (and it's a big 'if') God is all-powerful and wholly good; if he created the world and all that is in it, there's surely nothing to stop him from reconstituting our personalities after our physical death. In this way our souls — the 'you-ness' of you and the 'me-ness' of me — could be suitably recreated by God in a way which would be appropriate for the spiritual or heavenly afterlife with him. Those who argue against this that our bodies are destroyed at death by fire or worms are simply missing the point. An all-powerful God who loves his creatures could easily transform their individuality at death and make them fit for the spiritual existence which the Bible calls 'heaven'. As St Paul says, God will give us a 'spiritual body'. Whatever that is we don't know, but we can safely leave our puzzlement in the hands of the all-powerful, all-loving God.

Well that's all very well if we accept the doctrine of God's existence in the first place — if we're prepared to believe that what the Bible says about him is true. Now there are good reasons for believing the biblical account but there are good reasons against it as well. We'll look at the Bible as an authority (or not) in a later chapter.

The point I'd like to make here is that if we accept the biblical account of God and the afterlife as true, then we must take care that we understand what the Bible actually says and not simply interpret it in the most favourable or pleasing way to us. And we can't get away from the fact that, as well as talking about eternal happiness with God, the Bible also speaks of 'the outer darkness', 'the lake of fire', 'eternal torment' and 'everlasting punishment'. We're left in no doubt that the New Testament writers, and even Jesus himself, expected that some people will suffer these endless torments — hell (Matthew 5:13, 13:40-43, 25:46; Luke 16:23; Romans 6:23; Revelation 20:14-15, etc.). Whatever else may be said about biblical teaching, it's not cosy or comfortable. It speaks of a real heaven and of peace, love, forgiveness; but also of God's wrath, of fire and punishment, of 'weeping and gnashing of teeth'.

Many people are able to accept the biblical teaching. 'Well', they argue, 'there is a heaven and there is a hell. But God has shown us how to escape the latter and come to enjoy the former with him. This comes through the confession of our wrongdoings and our decision to live a life of complete trust in him. It's no use saying you haven't been warned!'

Those who disagree with this point of view — and they include the contributors to *Essays and Reviews* which we talked about at the beginning of this chapter — put forward quite a different sort of argument. It goes like this: 'Even I, an *imperfect* human being, would not (if it were in my power) allow anyone — even my worst enemy — to suffer *forever* in hell. How much less then would a perfect God allow such a thing?'

That might seem like an end of the dispute. But it isn't. The believer in eternal punishment counters the argument with something like this:

> That's all very well but God cannot go against his own nature. And his nature is all perfection. Therefore he cannot allow imperfection any part in the Kingdom of Heaven. He has given us the means to attain to perfection through faith in his son Jesus Christ. If we reject that faith then we cannot share the perfection. Moreover, God has given us a choice whether we believe or whether we do not believe. He will respect that choice (freewill). So if you decide not to believe then that's your 'privilege'. God will not overrule your freewill. Those who choose not heaven will find themselves having chosen hell.

In case you think this terrifying point of view is just one more doctrine invented by me for the sake of argument, let me assure you that there are many people in the churches who believe it literally. Take this passage for instance written not in 1860 but in 1970 by David Watson a clergyman in the Church of England:

> Christ makes it clear in His teaching that hell is a place of eternal separation from everything good, a place where a person will see that God is right and that he is wrong, and will know at last the glory of God — but that he can never experience it. In this story (Luke 16) Christ talks of 'a great chasm fixed', there is no second chance after death.

You can read more 'good news' ('Gospel' means 'good news') like that in the rest of Mr Watson's book: *My God is Real!* Certainly, if that sort of God is real then we have cause to tremble and quake. And David Watson isn't alone. There are many teachers of religion in our churches who would have us believe that most of us are on 'the primrose way to the everlasting bonfire' as the late great William Shakespeare once put it.

Perhaps the arguments in favour of hell fire and damnation, in favour of eternal separation from God break down for the very good reason that a perfect God will eventually see to it that his love triumphs over his wrath. That his willingness to forgive is greater than his need for simple justice. Certainly, I find a great deal that appeals in the argument: 'Even I, imperfect as I am, wouldn't allow anyone to suffer endless torment. How much less, then, would an all-perfect God permit such a thing.' But it's not up to me to tell you what to think. You should puzzle it out for yourselves. Arrange a debate or a trial. Tell a parable to illustrate your own view on the subject of eternal punishment.

Conclusion

The ideas of heaven and hell are naturally bound up with the doctrine of a life after death. We can't prove that there's a life after death any more than we can prove that God exists. But there's nothing unusual about this because strictly speaking we can't prove very much at all outside the concepts of pure mathematics. If you doubt this, try to prove that *you* exist to a classmate who has set himself to argue against you. Or try to prove that there is no tiger in the next room. Even that there is a next room!

Once again, I'd like to end the chapter on a personal note. Not so that you'll simply take what I say as gospel truth — but hopefully you won't dismiss it out of hand either. Rather so you'll have an alternative point of view to discuss, to pull to pieces even.

This, too is based on the idea of wonder. I know it's possible to argue that the universe is vast and we are very little; that we're puny and insignificant in comparison with the rest of the cosmos; that we're always in danger of falling prey to exaggerated ideas about our own importance in the whole scheme of things. I'm aware that it's extremely difficult to have any concept at all of what a person might be after the dissolution of his body. And that the idea of a 'soul' is a very woolly notion hard to imagine, impossible to define to everyone's satisfaction.

But I know this: the commonsense view of matter — that's tables and chairs, footballs and hockey sticks, boys and girls, men and women (at least the solid, touchable and visible parts of us) — is not the same view of matter held by modern physicists. Apparently all those ordinary everyday objects aren't as 'solid' as they appear. That goes for our bodies too. They're particles, infinitely small and whirling at an unimaginable speed. And wait, they're not even particles if what we mean by a 'particle' is a tiny blob of stuff. No, they're electrical charges or waves, sometimes. A noted physicist once said: 'Sub-atomic particles behave as particles on Monday, Wednesday and Friday; and on Tuesday, Thursday and Saturday like waves'. So it seems that the commonsense world of the senses is not at all as it appears. The philosopher Hugo Meynell said recently: 'When you actually come to grips with understanding the nature of all that out there (i.e. matter) it dissolves into mathematics'.

In other words, it's beginning to look as if matter isn't as material as was once thought. And if it's not material then what is it? Could it be some kind of mental or spiritual stuff? And if so, what price St Paul's 'spiritual body'? What price a new life after death which might turn out after all to be no more than an abrupt reorganization of 'mental stuff'? I'm offering no certainty since I'm far from certain myself and under such circumstances dogmatism of any kind is quite out of place. One thing is clear: the more we discover about the universe, the more mysterious and wonderful it seems to be. And there's no good reason to think that our present doctrines about its nature are anything but primitive and crude, early guesses. After all, the science and mathematics of 1980 bears little resemblance to the accepted opinions of 1880. The debate about life after death is by no means over. You might like to make your own contribution to it.

Exercise
(1) Why do you think the ideas of heaven and hell have emerged as part of so many religions the world over?
(2) Is there such a thing as 'the soul'?
(3) What makes you you *and me* me?
(4) If a belief is old (has been held for thousands of years) have we more or less reason for accepting it as true?
(5) Are we 'just our bodies'? If so, what do we mean by the word 'mind'?
(6) Does the fact that many people hope for a life after death make the belief in such an existence more or less convincing?
(7) If death is natural, why do we grieve?
(8) Was Pascal on a good bet?
(9) Would a God of love permit even the most evil of his creatures to suffer endless torment?
(10) What light, if any, does modern science throw on the concept of life after death?

3 Miracles

What is a miracle? The *Concise Oxford Dictionary* says it is a 'marvellous event due to some supernatural agency'. This means some extraordinary act performed by God and usually against or contradicting what we call the laws of nature. Do such events ever happen? Many religious people would claim that they do and that miracles are interventions in history by God himself to bring about his own purposes for the world.

For example, many Jewish people believe that:

> the people of Israel went into the midst of the sea on dry ground, the waters being a wall to them on their right hand and on their left. (Exodus 14:22)

This quotation is taken from the Old Testament part of the Bible, from the Book of Exodus which tells of the Jews' escape from Egypt. Many Jews believe that this escape was miraculous — that it was brought about by God who caused extraordinary events to occur so that his people might be set free from slavery.

You can read about many miracles in the first few chapters of Exodus. For instance the story is told that when God wanted to give his servant Moses courage and confidence to face Pharaoh, the King of Egypt, he:

> . . . said to him, 'what is that in your hand?' He said, 'A rod.' And God said, 'Cast it on the ground.' So he cast it on the ground, and it became a serpent; and Moses fled from it. But the Lord said to Moses, 'Put out your hand and take it by the tail' — so he put out his hand and caught it, and it became a rod in his hand — that they might believe . . . (Exodus 4:2-5)

'That they might believe.' All well and good. But do we believe? What can we make of such stories? The Old Testament is full of them. Let's have just two more examples — one spectacular, the other rather comical:

> And as they still went on and talked, behold, a chariot of fire and two horses of fire separated the two of them. And Elijah went up by a whirlwind into heaven. (2 Kings 2:11)

and on a lighter note perhaps:

> When the ass saw the angel of the Lord, she lay down under Balaam

and Balaam's anger was kindled, and he struck the ass with his staff. Then the Lord opened the mouth of the ass, and she said to Balaam, 'What have I done to you, that you have struck me these three times?' (Numbers 22:27 ff)

Chariots of fire? Talking donkeys? What can we make of such stories except that they are fanciful nonsense?

Then we come to the New Testament and to the miracles of Jesus. These are of various types. First there is the miracle of healing. Not just one, but many. One example will do to illustrate the sort of things which are supposed to have happened:

When Jesus came down from the mountain, great crowds followed him; and behold, a leper came to him and knelt before him, saying, 'Lord, if you will, you can make me clean.' And he stretched out his hand and touched him, saying, 'I will; be clean.' And immediately his leprosy was cleansed. (Matthew 8:1-3)

There are many stories of this kind where Jesus heals a sick person or even raises someone from the dead — see the story of Lazarus in St John's gospel, chapter 11.

Next we read about so-called nature miracles as on the occasion when Jesus is said to have turned water into wine (John 2:1-11) or in this account of the stilling of the storm:

And when the evening came, the boat was out on the sea, and Jesus was alone on the land. And he saw that they were distressed in rowing, for the wind was against them. And about the fourth watch of the night he came to them, walking on the sea. He meant to pass by them, but when they saw him walking on the sea they thought it was a ghost and cried out, for they all saw him and were terrified. But immediately he spoke to them and said, 'Take heart, it is I; have no fear.' And he got into the boat with them and the wind ceased. (Mark 6:47-51)

Finally there are the miracle stories about what God did to Jesus himself. You know he was put to death on the first Good Friday. Well, according to the gospel writers, that wasn't the end of the story:

Mary stood weeping outside the tomb, and as she wept she stooped to look into the tomb; and she saw two angels in white, sitting where the body of Jesus had lain, one at the head and one at the feet. They said to her, 'Woman why are you weeping?' She said to them, 'Because they have taken away my Lord and I do not know where they have laid him.' Saying this, she turned round and saw Jesus standing there . . . (John 20:11-14)

But it would be a mistake to think that it is only the Bible which contains accounts of miracles. Miracle stories are a part of most religions and as far as the Christian faith goes, they didn't cease where the Bible ended. The lives of the saints are filled with remarkable stories. So one Elogios who lived about 1,650 years ago was:

> . . . struck by a passion for eternal things and deserted the world's hubbub. But he grew lonely; met a cripple and promised God that he would look after him till he died. The cripple after fifteen years fell sick. Elogios . . . cured him.

Then there are the stories of miraculous cures at Lourdes where St Bernadette claimed to have seen visions of the Virgin Mary. Pilgrims make the trek there to this day in the hope of being cured of their ailments.

And it is not only Jews and Christians who relate miraculous stories. They form part of most world religions. So Royston Pike tells us in a book about gods and heroes that Krishna, the Hindu god:

> . . . was so handsome that all the maidens fell in love with him, and he married seven or eight of them. Once on one of his rambles he met a crooked girl, and because she was so kind to him he made her as straight as a young tree. He fought and killed in single combat many a giant and ogre. He put the demons to flight.

Similar tales are told of gods and their prophets in all the religions of the world. What are we to make of these tales? Should we dismiss them with a polite smile or even with a sophisticated sneer?

The Beliefs of Barbarians?

It is commonly argued that all the miracles which were ever alleged to have taken place happened in primitive times to simple-minded people who had no knowledge of science and therefore would 'believe anything'. Certainly there is something to be said for this argument, but careful distinctions need to be made. Do you remember we accepted the dictionary's definition of a miracle as something which has a supernatural cause? Well it is more than likely that many of the ancient stories we read were never thought to be miracles in the first place but were simply remarkable tales from the past which people had exaggerated. These tales are sometimes called legends. What is a legend and how does it develop? Take the case of King Arthur and his Knights of the Round Table. Perhaps there was once such a king or hero and maybe he gathered around him a band of loyal followers. It is quite possible that they devoted themselves to noble causes such as protecting innocent women and children and defending religion.

But over a period of four or five hundred years or so — a period when there are few books and hardly anyone can read in any case — these stories soon became blown up out of all proportion. So the innocent women became enchantresses and the defence of religion is turned into a magical quest for the Holy Grail.

Perhaps there was once a famous outlaw called Robin Hood. Occasionally he was known to give some of his swag to the poor people. So in the popular mind he becomes, over a period of centuries, the honourable opponent of the wicked sheriff — and the darling of the ordinary people. What I'm trying to say here is that many of the stories which at first glance look like accounts of the miraculous may originally have been no more than good stories which became exaggerated — 'embroidered' as they say.

Perhaps this is true in the case of Balaam's ass. Maybe it simply sat down and would go no further because its rider was asking too much of it. After all, asses are quite famous for this kind of behaviour. Later, in the popular religious tradition, the story developed into an account of how God actually caused it to speak as a rebuke to its master who was going against God's will.

As it happens, that story of the parting of the Red Sea at the time of the Exodus from Egypt gives us a good example of what may have been a significant but not entirely unusual event becoming transformed into a full blown 'miracle' — not really a miracle at all. It is widely believed that much of the Old Testament was built out of four distinct traditions which go by the initials, 'J', 'D', 'E' and 'P'. 'J' is the earliest of these and 'P' is the latest. In between come 'E' and 'D'. Some think 'E' is earliest, but that's not so important for our present purposes. What is interesting is that this theory lets us see the whole account of the parting of the Red Sea in quite a different perspective. And Exodus chapter 14 no longer looks like a single account but like a development of at least three different traditions. First, 'J':

> the Lord drove the sea back by a strong east wind all night, and made the sea dry land, and the waters were divided. (Exodus 14:21)

So at first the actual facts of the case may have been no more than that there was an unusually strong wind which caused a low tide and the religious Jews interpreted this as God's doing. More dramatic perhaps, but not all that different at bottom from the parson who remarks smilingly, 'Ah I see the Lord has given us a fine day for the garden party!' Secondly, 'E':

> Lift up your rod, and stretch out your hand over the sea and divide it, that the people of Israel may go on dry ground through the sea. (Exodus 14:16)

This later part of the tradition makes the dry ground a result of a wonder done by Moses through the power of God. More 'miraculous' than the earlier 'J' account, but not yet the fully developed explanation of 'P' writing centuries later:

> And the people of Israel went into the midst of the sea on dry ground, the waters being a wall to them on their right hand and

on their left. (Exodus 14:22)

So, like the game of Chinese Whisper played around the classroom, original messages became exaggerated and even distorted. These are not miracles in the true sense then, but legends — exciting stories from the past made more exciting still by writers who have an interest in accounting for the events of the past in terms of God's special action on behalf of his people. After all, the writers of the Old Testament were religious Jews, committed to their faith in God and to telling others about him. Still, it's important to see that, even so, the Old Testament doesn't talk about 'miracles' as such but about 'mighty acts of God'.

But there is no doubt that many ancient peoples believed in a universe which was something like this:

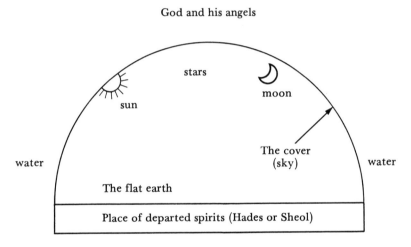

This is the so-called 'pre-scientific' view of an age which knew nothing of telescopes and circumnavigation. Perhaps 'pre-scientific' is a rather rude and in any case inaccurate description of this way of thinking. For it was scientific as far as it went. In an age without motorized sailing vessels or advanced technological gadgets, such a view of the world was genuinely scientific — if we mean by 'scientific' that which satisfactorily explains our experiences. There is nothing immediately nonsensical about the view that since there is a world, it must have been made by somebody or something — let us call that agent God. And, apart from mountains and valleys, the earth *looks* flat and not like a ball. The blue sky *looks* solid. And where else should departed spirits go since we do, after all, bury our dead in the ground? And surely there is water above the earth, or else where does the rain come from? No, 'pre-scientific' is inaccurate. 'Primitive science' is better. But who's to say that another two thousand years of history might not show our own so-called 'modern science' as equally primitive? But more of that later.

Let's just pause and see how far we've come in this chapter:

(1) To the conclusion that many so-called 'miracles' are really legendary accounts of historical events.

(2) That earlier civilizations were much more conscious of living in a world which was created by and under the direct control of God.

It follows from (2) that earlier peoples would not have the same problems about miracles that we have. If God made the world — and any other explanation was unthinkable — then surely he can do with it as he likes! And so where we begin in trying to decide what miracles are, if indeed they are possible at all, depends on our acceptance first of a particular interpretation of the world — a particular 'story'. If we accept, say, the first-century view of the world indicated in the drawing, we should find no difficulty in believing that God could 'send' his 'Son' (Jesus Christ) into the world from 'out there'; that Jesus could be born miraculously (of a virgin); that he should work many miracles himself (as God's Son); that he should finally rise from the dead and 'ascend' into heaven. Even that one day he may 'come again in power and great glory'. If we do not accept this particular 'story' as an explanation or interpretation of the world then we shall not be likely to accept miraculous incidents as events which actually happen.

The philosopher David Hume, whom we met in the first chapter, didn't accept the first-century world view or 'story'. He argued in *Dialogues:*

> It forms a strong presumption against all supernatural and miraculous relations, that they are observed chiefly to abound among ignorant and barbarous nations; or if a civilised people has ever given admission to any of them, that people will be found to have received them from ignorant and barbarous ancestors . . .

Is it possible then for an intellegent human being living in the last quarter of the twentieth century to believe that miracles occur? Or should the whole idea be despatched to the rag-bag of all our-of-date notions such as the flat earth and the water above the sky?

Recognizing Miracles

The first problem we have after 'when is a miracle not a miracle?' answer: 'when it's a legend' is of how to be sure that what we call a miracle has acutally taken place. Remember we defined a miracle as 'a marvellous event due to some supernatural agency'. Now many ancient peoples would, and actually did, believe that eclipses of the sun were miraculous occurrences.

Modern science reveals that these are rather the result of occasional conjunctions of the sun, the moon and the earth so that a shadow is cast, etc.

Now suppose that sometime in the not too distant future, say, next week, someone should drop a large book such as *A Concise History of the World*. And suppose that, instead of proceeding to the floor as it has done in every other case when it has been allowed to slip off the desk, it remains stationary for a moment or two in the air — and then falls. Would we not be tempted to say we had observed a miracle? It would appear that something had happened outside the description of natural causes. So the event must have been due to the operation of some 'supernatural agency'. Therefore, according to our definition, a miracle has occurred. But wait a minute. A primitive man could not have explained an eclipse without recourse to terms which, to us, are miraculous. Modern science can explain eclipses easily and simply and clearly. No 'supernatural agency' is involved. Might it not be possible then that in our *A Concise History of the World'*, which momentarily refuses to fall, there is not a supernatural agency at work but simply a natural agency whose nature we don't yet understand?

This is not at all far-fetched. Once we didn't understand magnetism; now there is a textbook explanation within reach of the understanding of every secondary-school child. Ask any high energy physicist if he can explain to you exactly what an atom is made of. He won't be able to do it. But he might be able in ten or twenty years time — or his great grandson might in 2053.

So we cannot say with certainty of any event which might happen whether or not it is a miracle according to our definition of its being 'due to some supernatural agency'. All we can say in the face of such an event as the floating *A Concise History of the World* or the President of the International Football Federation suddenly becoming invisible, or someone rising from the dead is that *at this moment in time* (as the Americans say for 'just now') we have no natural or scientific explanation for such events. Which is not to deny that one day we might come across such an explanation. But . . .

Are Miracles Possible?

This is easier asked than answered, because we use the word 'possible' in at least two ways. First, we apply it to statements in logic and mathematics. So we would say: 'In the way we normally do arithmetic, it is not possible for 2 + 2 to make 5'. Or 'In what we mean by logic, it is not possible for a married man to be a bachelor'. Therefore if anyone said, '2 + 2 = 5' or 'a bachelor is a married man' we should say he was contradicting himself.

For all we know, there may be languages in which 2 + 2 can add up to 5 and in which a married man can be called a bachelor, but in the way that we use logic and language these sentences are not possible. Philosophers say that they are logically contradictory. To say them and mean them is simply to say something and then unsay the same thing. This isn't a crime of course; it's just not very helpful.

Now let us look at the statement: 'Miracles are possible'. Clearly this is not logically contradictory. Anyone saying it does not say and unsay the same thing. But there are thousands of statements which, though not logically contradictory, we would want to call 'impossible'. This brings us to our second use of 'possible' and 'impossible'. For instance, 'My friend Christine is coming on the next train'. There's nothing logically contradictory about that and in the normal course of events we might look at the timetable, check the calendar to make sure today is a Wednesday and then, remembering that Christine often comes on this particular train on Wednesday, say: 'Yes it's quite *possible* that Christine will be on the next train.' And by 'possible' we don't mean *logically possible* but 'likely'.

The fact is that our second way of using 'possible' is usually just another way of saying that a particular event is likely. So there are lots of statements we would say are not possible in the sense that they are extremely unlikely. For example: 'Pigs will fly' — not likely! 'The Hot Air Balloon Party will win the next General Election' — not likely. Notice, both these events are possible in the sense that to suggest they might occur does not involve the speaker in a logical contradiction. His hearers will merely conclude that he has been sitting in the sun for too long and he has turned a little crazy. But let them try to *prove* before the event that either pigs will never fly or that it is beyond the bounds of possibility for the Hot Air Balloon Party to win the General Election. No such proof is possible. Anything *might* happen. It's just that we reckon some events to be so unlikely that we say they are not possible, impossible.

Some people think that miracles come into this category. For while it is no contradiction to say 'miracles can happen' it has been thought by many to be an extremely unlikely statement. So unlikely that in an offhand and imprecise way, people sometimes say 'miracles are impossible'. Let's look at some of the reasons for this disbelief or scepticism. David Hume was firmly against the idea that there are miracles and he wrote some very strong words in defence of his argument. I'll quote him from time to time — partly because he writes in such an entertaining style.

Barbarians Again?

Hume wrote in *Enquiry Concerning the Human Understanding:*

> Nothing is so convenient as a decisive argument . . . which must at least *silence* the most arrogant bigotry and superstition, and free us from their impertinent solicitations. I flatter myself that I have discovered an argument of like nature, which, if just, will, with the wise and learned, be an everlasting check to all kinds of superstitious delusion, and consequently, will be useful as long as the world endures.

For so long, I presume, will the accounts of miracles and prodigies be found in all history, sacred and profane.

Well let us look at this argument that David Hume flatters himself on having found. He reckons that all our knowledge about things that happen in the world is based on experience. But even experience is not infallible. Sometimes our senses deceive us. So we have to count up our experiences and decide which interpretation of them is the most probable. For instance, if rain fell nine out of ten of the times that clouds appeared we should have good reason from experience of thinking that the next time it's cloudy it will probably rain. We infer that it will rain on the basis of our experience of seeing together cloud and rain so often.

Now Hume says:

> The reason why we place any credit in witnesses and historians, is not derived from any connection which we perceive *a priori*, between testimony and reality, but because we are accustomed to find a conformity between them.

In other words, the only good reason for believing anyone's account of anything is that such an account does not run contrary to our general experience. The words 'general experience' are important because Hume is basing his whole argument against miracles on probability — and we decide how probable any event's occurrence is on our general experience. Hume goes on:

> But when the fact attested is such a one as has seldom fallen under our observation, here is a contest of two opposite experiences . . . The incredibility of a fact, it was allowed, might invalidate . . . an authority.

In other words, if someone comes and tells us that, for instance, a man has risen from the dead then what that someone says is part of our experience. But it is a much more general part of our experience that men do not rise from the dead, so our general experience outweighs the particular witness.

Look how Hume strengthens his argument about miracles by introducing the concept of the laws of nature:

> A miracle is a violation of the laws of nature; and as a firm and unalterable experience has established these laws, the proof against a miracle, from the very nature of the fact, is as entire as any argument from experience can possibly be imagined.

This argument is not, perhaps, as convincing as David Hume hoped it might be when he wrote that bit about its being 'useful as long as the world endures'. For what he seems to be saying is simply that miracles cannot occur because miracles cannot occur. And this of course is no kind of proof at all. But it's not obvious at first glance, so let's look at Hume's argument of that last quotation in stages:

(1) He defines a miracles as 'a violation of the laws of nature'. And how do we know what the laws of nature are? Hume answers:

(2) They are based on 'a firm and unalterable experience'. Therefore:

(3) Miracles cannot happen because they are against experience.

What Hume takes no account of is that the so-called 'laws of nature' are not firm and unalterable. In fact science finds exceptions quite regularly to these laws. And the method of science is to incorporate exceptions into the laws themselves. For example, suppose we take the scientific hypothesis: 'Steel doesn't float'. But then we see a floating battleship so we are forced to alter the original hypothesis to accommodate this new discovery. Perhaps we say then 'steel doesn't float *except* etc . . .'

There is another point against Hume: everything that happens must be either natural or unnatural. If we define miracles as violations of the laws of nature — as Hume does — then they cannot be natural. So either there are no such things as miracles or else, if they occur, they are unnatural. Hume cannot have things both ways. He cannot say that miracles do not occur because everything that occurs is natural without first demonstrating that it would be impossible for anything unnatural or supernatural to occur. And Hume nowhere proves that supernatural events cannot or do not occur. He simply states that they don't by defining everything that happens as natural.

This won't do at all because everyone knows that anyone can define anything as it suits him — like Humpty Dumpty who said: 'When I use a word, it means exactly what I want it to mean — no more and no less'. If we all were to behave like that, we'd soon all be speaking different languages. It is important that we agree on the meanings of words, on what we mean when we use them. Just imagine the chaotic consequences which would arise if everyone accepted the definition: 'This page is the Sunday lunch!' Hume's definitions of 'natural' and 'unalterable experience' are more cleverly concealed examples of the same kind of thing — defining an object as we wish.

The Problem of Evidence

Hume says all knowledge about the world comes to us through the experience of our senses. And he maintains this has always been true. It follows that, if it ever happened at all, the first reports of the resurrection of Jesus must have been based on someone's sense experience. Someone must have seen Jesus alive again, if, as I say, the resurrection actually happened — otherwise, since all knowledge comes through sense experience, no one could ever claim to know of the resurrection. Hume says our experience of an ancient miracle like the resurrection (if it ever happened) is based on our senses. That is hearing the word which has been passed down the years: 'Jesus is risen from the dead'. From this Hume goes on to argue that the experiences which we have *directly* today do not include appearances of men risen from the dead. Therefore, we must reject as mere hearsay the reports of the resurrection because we only have them on the basis of *indirect* or second-hand evidence. In Hume's own words: 'A weaker evidence can never destroy a stronger'.

As we have seen, this is only true if we will admit the existence of those events alone which accord with our experience. Frequently, we have no direct experience of an event but we believe it happened just the same. It is not the case that in my direct daily experience there are battles of Marston Moor. But I believe there was once a Battle of Marston Moor because the history books tell me so and just up the road from where I live there is a monument to the 1644 battle.

Many things which happen today were thought impossible a hundred years ago. Take wireless messages or walking on the face of the moon as a couple of instances. Might it not be possible at least that certain events which do not appear to occur today might have happened in the past? I'm not saying they did occur — only that we should not dismiss the possibility of their occurrence. And how does Hume's argument from experience account for unique events? Unique events are those things which happen only once. If there is a God, and neither Hume nor anyone else has ever proved that there isn't, might he not have raised one man from the dead on one occasion and isn't it therefore at least possible that this man was Jesus Christ? Once again, I'm not saying it all happened as the Bible says it did. I'm only asking whether such a miracle can be disproved. Certainly, in what we've seen so far David Hume has not disproved miracles. He has put forward some arguments which those who believe in miracles are obliged to try and refute. I think the case goes against Hume for the reasons given already and also because he has not disproved supernatural causation. That is the existence of miracles worked by God.

Wishful Thinking

Do you remember when Uri Geller was all the rage with his ability to bend spoons? And what about the interest in UFOs which made a film like *Close Encounters of the Third Kind* so popular? Ordinary people don't normally bend spoons — at least not unless they touch them. And most of us have never seen a flying saucer — outside the kitchen. Isn't it possible then that people believe in Geller and UFOs because they want to believe? Perhaps because the world seems more interesting if spoons can bend by magic or unknown forces and if creatures from another galaxy are observing us. In other words isn't all this sort of thing what we call 'wishful thinking'? And aren't miracles part of the same thing? This may be true. But let's get one thing clear. The cause of a belief has nothing to do with the existence or non-existence of the object of that belief. For example, I may see stars because I've been knocked on the head. The fact that I've been knocked on the head doesn't affect the existence of stars though! I might believe in miracles because I want them to be true. Lots of other people, perhaps including David Hume, may not want them to be true. The point is that either wanting or not wanting has nothing to do with whether there are in fact such occurrences as miracles.

This is an argument which comes up time after time. Some say, 'Our idea of God comes from our idea of our human father'. Perhaps it does? In any case, why deny it? For it remains true that wherever the idea came from originally, it has nothing to do with the existence or non-existence of God in fact. This is worth emphasizing because as an argument it deceived even so great a great thinker as the psychologist Sigmund Freud.

A Good Lie?

Some argue as follows: 'Religion is generally speaking a good thing. It makes people behave themselves and is good for public order. But the people will only believe in religion if we can tell them that it is derived from miraculous tales. Now we know that the miraculous tales are false, but let us pretend that they are true so that they will be believed and public order will be maintained.' In other words, it is argued, the miracle stories are kinds of 'white lies' — they aren't true but the pretence that they're true does more good than the fact that they're not. So let us have the pretence rather than the truth. Perhaps you would like to discuss whether this particular approach could ever be justified.

But whatever you decide in the end doesn't have any effect on whether miracles really happen (or happened) or not. We saw that the cause of a belief is, as the philosophers say, independent of the truth of a belief. In the same way the reasons for the advancement of a particular belief — that belief in miracles and wondrous tales is good for morality for instance — have nothing to do with whether the belief itself is true or false.

So we may end this section with the general statement: that the causes or purposes of a belief (in miracles) are not connected to the truth or falsity of that belief.

Supernatural vs Natural

We've seen that some of the things which a century ago would have been regarded as miracles — television for instance — are today taken for granted. More precisely, that they can be explained in terms of natural science. And we see how this makes it difficult for us ever to be sure that a genuine miracle has taken place. It might be simply a marvellous and rare event which, although we can't account for it today, science may well give a perfectly good explanation of it tomorrow. Take a case of apparently miraculous healing.

In the early 1970s in Scotland a man was dying of cancer. The illness was so advanced that his doctor didn't think he would survive for more than a day. In this particular case there was no prospect of a cure. The patient's family said prayers for his recovery to a saint of the church. Next day, there was a full and perfect recovery. This was vouched for by doctors and specialists. And the Pope declared that a miracle had taken place. That God — a supernatural agent — had intervened and brought about the cure.

Well, what is not in doubt is that the man's disease, usually fatal, disappeared overnight. But was this really a supernatural event, divine intervention, a miracle? Or was it a mysterious but non-miraculous incidence of the body healing itself? Perhaps one day science may explain this strange occurrence and many others like it. Maybe we shall never know how the cure came about. We are presented with a choice between two unknowns:

(1) An unexplainable supernatural cure.
(2) An unexplainable natural cure.

The choice is a straight one. Which kind of unknown do you prefer — the one which is a result of possible divine intervention or the other which is a working of nature which as yet we don't understand?

Miracles as Signs

The New Testament frequently speaks of miracles as signs. That is they are not important in themselves. Their true value is that they serve to convince us that God is in charge of the world, that he is Lord of nature and of history. So, for instance, the story in St John's Gospel about Jesus turning the water into wine is an illustration — a visual aid if you like — of God's newer and richer revelation of himself in the person of Jesus. Jesus himself sometimes became impatient with his disciples when they asked for miracles. 'Except you see signs and wonders', he said, 'you will not believe.' At other times he was more patient and, according to the New Testament account, performed miracles, 'that you [the disciples] might believe'.

Some scholars go further than this and say that as a matter of fact the miracle stories of the New Testament didn't really happen at all. They were dramatized or acted parables. Like the parables, they were stories with a message. So when we come to study the accounts of Jesus' resurrection from the dead, these scholars say we shouldn't look for an actual resurrection but that we should interpret the word 'resurrection' to mean that at a suitable distance in time after Jesus' death the disciples realized what he had been trying to teach them and they experienced new life — resurrection life. You know how people sometimes say when they understand something for the first time 'Ah, I've cottoned on' or 'The penny's dropped'? Well, according to some scholars the story about the resurrection simply amounts to the fact that with the disciples the penny had dropped about the meaning and purpose of Jesus' life and teaching. This enabled them in some measure to share the quality of life which Jesus possessed. So they expressed this by saying that Jesus had risen from the dead. This explanation of the resurrection satisfies some Christians.

Others are less happy about it. They say that if the disciples had simply meant that the penny had dropped then they would simply have said, 'The penny has dropped' or expressed the same thing in a similar way. And it is argued, something must have happed to change those frightened men and women which made them willing to risk life and limb for the sake of their message. Many Christians say that something was the resurrection of Jesus from the tomb. That it really happened. That it was a special act of God. A miracle. Further, they say that unless the resurrection really happened the disciples would never have had the ability and the confidence to preach and teach as they did. And that no one is prepared to risk his life for what he knows to be a lie. The issue is far from settled. What do you think?

Why No Regular Miracles?

Let's suppose that there is a God. And it is just as reasonable to believe that someone made the world, that there is some rational mind behind it, than that it all just came about by accident — isn't it? Then why doesn't this all-powerful God work his miracles more often — to avert earthquakes and to stop car crashes for instance? Well there is one answer to this question which we shall look at in more detail in Chapter 5 on 'Evil'. But another answer is that God works miracles only occasionally as hints of his presence, as guideposts or signposts. He doesn't bludgeon his way into human history by suspending the so-called 'laws of nature' every five minutes, but saves his miracles for special revelations — like the incarnation (becoming man) and resurrection of his Son.

Besides, have you ever thought, if God worked miracles all the time — stopped every car crash, caught every falling person in mid-air — then these events would no longer appear to be miracles but only the natural sequence of things! And we should have no use for the word 'miracle' at all. By definition miracles are exceptional events. They are out of the ordinary. Perhaps they don't occur at all? Maybe they're simply flukes or freaks of chance and nature? One thing's certain — if the person who believes in miracles has a hard task to justify his belief, the non-believer has an equally difficult job in accounting for 'miraculous appearances'.

Exercise
(1) Make up your own definition of the word 'miracle'.
(2) According to this chapter, what's the difference between a miracle and a legend?
(3) If you were to shake a dice six times and three turned up on each occasion would that be a miracle? If three turned up a hundred times in succession would that be a miracle?
(4) Could God cause a donkey to talk?
(5) When Uri Geller bends spoons and stops watches from ticking is he working miracles? If so, how do you know? If not, how does he do it?

(Don't say simply 'by a trick'!)

(6) *'Even God cannot do the logically impossible. He cannot make a piece of material which is all wood and all steel at the same time.' Can he?*

(7) *Say what we mean by the two uses of 'possible' to be found in this chapter.*

(8) *State one of David Hume's arguments against miracles. Do you agree with him?*

(9) *Are the laws of nature firm and unalterable?*

(10) *If a man makes a dramatic recovery from a usually fatal illness, might this be a miracle?*

(11) *'Miracles don't happen. They're just wishful thinking.' Debate this statement.*

(12) *Which is it more reasonable to believe:*
  (a) *The Christian faith spread because the disciples witnessed Jesus' resurrection from the dead?*
  (b) *The Christian faith spread because the disciples 'cottoned on' to a new kind of life?*

(13) *Is it nonsense to say: 'Everything is a miracle'?*

(14) *Sit and think in silence for three minutes — everybody. Take a vote on whether you believe miracles occur:*

  (a) *very occasionally;*   (c) *often;*
  (b) *sometimes;*   (d) *never.*

(15) *Suppose that Jesus really rose from the dead. How would you tell whether this was a miracle (that it was supernaturally caused) or that it was the sort of thing that could happen naturally — only, say, once in a million years?*

4 Religion and Science

The story has got around that religion is false and out of date. That it has been disproved by science. We notice that even professors of theology and religion sometimes seem to agree with this view. So as we have seen, Rudolf Bultmann, Professor at Marburg, used to say of the miracle stories of the New Testament: 'You can't believe that sort of thing in an age of electric light and the wireless'.

Others argue that scientists are merely being presumptuous when they claim to be able to answer questions which are the traditional concern of religion. Questions like: 'Is there a God?' and 'Does the human personality survive death?' Whichever side you take, or even if you keep quiet and simply listen to the arguments, you'll soon find yourself involved in deep controversies when the issue of science versus religion is being discussed.

It's well known that unproductive arguments most commonly arise when people use words without first saying clearly what they mean by them. To take an apparently trivial example from, say, the world of football, you might get the following result:

Jack: It says here that City's performance was average.

Jill: That's a load of rubbish, I saw the game and they played well. They always play well.

Jack: Yes. I think that's what the reporter means. They played their average game.

Jill: Look, there's nothing average about City. They're great.

James: What about when they lost to United then?

Jack: Well I'd say United played above average on that day.

James: But United are only half way up the League, so they must be just an average side.

Jill: United? They're pathetic! Not even an average second division side . . .

This kind of conversation goes on all the time. Sometimes the participants become very heated. But the reason for their apparently violent disagreement arises out of the fact that they're all using the word 'average' in a different way. Look at just some of the meanings this word has, depending on context:

(1) Average — about 50%. Not outstandingly good but not particularly poor either.

(2) Average — only average or not much good.
(3) Average — a good average or better than some.
(4) Average — average for the league United or City are in.
(5) Average — average for them or up to their own usual expectations.
and then there's the vaguest of all:
(6) Average — normal.

Two vague words for the price of one. And it's vague words that cause most of the trouble in arguments. Words whose meanings are not immediately clear. Once again, if I say, 'There are a few peanuts in this pocket' someone else might disagree with me not simply by saying, 'No, the bag is empty'. He might say, 'I don't call that many "a few". There are ten in there. Ten's a lot!' On the other hand he could say, 'That's not even a few. There are only three nuts there'.

It's obvious that in cases where the word is precise the scope for argument is less. For instance, if I'd said, 'There are precisely *six* peanuts in that bag' then the area of dispute would have been considerably narrowed at once. The trouble is that most of the words we consider to be really important are vague. How do we agree on just what we mean by 'good'? Look at the way people disagree about who or what is 'beautiful' or 'handsome'. In just the same way the word 'God' means so many different things to lots of different people. How difficult it is then to talk about God and religion and whether these are in conflict with science until we agree on what we mean by the words we're using.

What do we Mean by 'Religion'?

Even a small dictionary tells us that it comes from a Latin word connected with the verb 'to bind'. Then it goes on to offer five different shades of meaning:
(1) Monastic condition, being monk or nun.
(2) Practice of sacred rites.
(3) One of the prevalent systems of faith and worship.
(4) Human recognition of superhuman controlling power . . .
(5) Action that one is bound to do . . . Make a religion of doing.

No doubt the larger dictionaries have even more to say on the subject. But five definitions are more than we need to provide us with all the ammunition for a mighty row based on misunderstanding. Not everyone who is religious is a monk or a nun. What about the local vicar or the churchwardens? Candidates for confirmation are religious aren't they? And if you're saying the Lord's Prayer in school assembly isn't that being religious as well? So definition number 1 can lead to confusion.

Number 2 is just as vague. Tribes in New Guinea practise sacred rites. So do the local Roman Catholics at Mass on Sunday morning. But neither group would belong with the other. Quakers are very religious and yet they practise no sacred rites at all.

To call a religion a 'prevalent system of faith and worship' (number 3) isn't satisfactory. Prevalent in Russia or China? Jehovah's Witnesses and Christian Scientists claim to be religious but they are greatly outnumbered in many countries by devotees of other religions. So they cannot claim to be prevalent.

While most religious people believe in God, number 4 is perhaps not strictly accurate, for many Buddhists (who are certainly religious people) do not admit the existence of a 'superhuman controlling power'. And number 5 is perhaps the most vague definition of all and therefore the least satisfactory since it allows almost any act to count as 'religious'. You might say, 'He gets up every morning at six, without fail, religiously' or even, 'She makes a religion out of avoiding Church'.

Before we can go any further in our comparison and discussion of religion and science we must come to some genuine idea of what we mean by 'religion'. Our definition need not be too restrictive but it must avoid being so vague as to spoil proper and reasonable discussion.

Belief or Attitude?

A belief is something for which we are prepared to give reasons:
'It will, I believe, be a fine day tomorrow.'
'Why?'
'Because the forecast was good and the barometer is rising.'
    An attitude may simply be held without any particular reason:
'I don't like her.'
'Why not?'
'No reason specially. I just don't like her.'
    Sometimes religion seems to be a series of beliefs. For instance, that there is a God; that he made the world; that he loves his creation. At other times it may have more of the characteristics of an attitude. People talk about 'feeling' religious and about 'religious experience'. Some churchpeople will tell you that they go to church because they believe certain doctrines to be true. Others don't stress the doctrines so much as their own emotions. They go to church because that makes them feel good. Even the feelings themselves may have nothing at all to do with what the church teaches as true or false. So it's possible to have attitudes and feelings without having to give reasons for them. But is it possible to have even attitudes without there is a cause for the attitudes? And in the case of religion isn't the cause of religious attitudes none other than God himself? One problem arising out of this question is that of deciding (if God is responsible for religious attitudes) who or what is the cause of attitudes which are non-religious? In short, if God exists and reveals himself to some people through their feelings, then why doesn't he reveal himself in the same way to all people?

Religious Experience — The Numinous

Some have suggested that there is a certain class of experiences common to all which may properly be called religious experiences or feelings of awe and dread. These are said to be experiences of the numinous. You'll recognize this kind of thing instantly. Think of stories that begin in darkness and thunderstorm and feature the ominous plod of an invisible giant creature. Or the appearance on a calm and moonlit night of a ghost ship. Steps descending into an ancient tomb. Film and television people are quick to exploit our experiences of awe and dread as they produce even more gory and scary versions of *The Curse of the Mummy's Tomb* and *Dracula*.

Perhaps you can remember as a young child being strangely attracted to and yet frightened by certain fairy tales? This is an example of the numinous — awe and dread. And the popularity of such films as *The Exorcist* and *The Omen* shows that our experiences of the numinous, of being attracted to what is terrifying, are shared by almost everyone. This does not mean, of course, that these experiences are proofs of God's existence. We saw in Chapter 3 on Miracles that the cause of a belief is not in itself a reason in support of the truth of a belief. But we might ask ourselves questions about the nature of these experiences of awe and dread since they are shared by all men and women. Is it possible, at least, to consider the traditional belief that the cause of our religious experiences is none other than the supreme religious subject — God himself?

Certain objections to this view are plain to see. First, it might be argued that these feelings of awe and dread — so-called religious experiences — are hangovers from a primitive and unscientific age. Men and women were naturally afraid in a world whose workings they couldn't understand. Secondly, there's the view that these feelings have their origin not outside us but within. They arise as by-products of the way we function. You know all the sayings about the cheese eaten at night making for bad dreams. And Scrooge's statement to Marley's ghost: 'There's more gravy than grave about you!' Thirdly, there is the undeniable fact that while the feelings themselves are real, and no doubt have very real causes, we cannot simply proceed to identify those causes with God.

To sum up, religious experiences of awe and dread may arise out of primitive superstitions which we're gradually getting rid of. Or they may be caused by the activities of our own bodies and brains. Finally they may have causes about which we know little at the moment but which are not in principle undiscoverable.

The reason I have written at such length about these feelings is because while religion has to do with beliefs and rationality it is also connected with attitudes and the irrational or non-rational. Any phenomenon which is so widespread as the feelings of awe and dread must be considered in trying to say what we mean by 'religion' because there is a powerful argument which says that all our religious ideas have their beginning in these feelings. Certainly, a scientific approach to religion which did *not* consider this aspect would be less than satisfactory.

But religion also makes certain claims about the nature and purpose of the universe, its creation by God and so on. Christianity, in particular, does this. We should examine the nature of these claims and see whether they conflict with the claims of science. First we must look at the meaning of the other problem word in the title of this chapter — science.

Scientific Method

Science is a method which began as an art or a skill. Greeks called science *tekne* — a word from which we get 'technology'. So science isn't simply thinking or theorising in the abstract; it is 'doing something'. Thucydides (471-400 B.C.) gives an account of his scientific approach to medicine:

> Anyone, physician or layman, may say what he thinks about the probable origin of the plague, and the causes which he thinks were enough to produce so great a disorder. I, for my part, shall describe only what it was like, and record those symptoms which might enable it to be recognized again, if ever it should recur; for I was attacked by it myself, and personally observed others who suffered from it.

Notice the words 'describe only what it was like and record those symptoms which might enable it to be recognized again'. This is the crux of scientific method. Avoiding all airy-fairy speculations and concentrating on hard physical evidence. Noting. Measuring. Counting. Listing. Doctors who use the scientific method don't try to explain the facts of the case or the appearances by recourse to such speculations as 'It's the will of the gods' or 'It's a punishment for sin'. Like all other scientists they observe what is actually there and try and limit themselves to natural or physical explanations based on past experience.

Let's take an example — not from medicine this time but from an ordinary everyday and every year event. It's your job to find a tub or a pot for the Christmas tree. You naturally want the right size. Not too shallow, or else the tree would overbalance; not too deep, or the tree would be dominated by the excessive volume of the tub and not look 'right'. The first question you might reasonably ask yourself is: 'Which tub did I use last year?' This is an example of simple science. In the jargon you are: 'Reproducing previously validated conditions in order to achieve similarity of results'. Or in plain English you're going on past experience.

Of course, the first time you set up the Christmas tree you had no past experience to go on. So what did you do then? Simply proceed by trial and error. Try one pot. Tree topples. Conclusion: too small. Try another pot. Tree planted all right but you can hardly get in the lounge for the bulkiness of the pot. Conclusion: too big. After a few trials you might find a pot which is just right. Think of Goldilocks and the three bears and that inquisitive young lady's experiments with the porridge, the chairs and the beds. These are simplified examples of scientific method. In the laboratory every attempt is made to be much more careful and accurate, precise and exact.

Hypothesis and Experiment

A hypothesis is a kind of formalized bet. And an experiment might be pictured as a race at the end of which you find out whether or not your hypothesis is a winner. Let's graduate from the simple task of planting Christmas trees. Suppose you are a modern psychologist and therefore, for highly important reasons best known to yourself, you wish to discover which way rats will turn in a maze. Perhaps if you're able to find out which way they turn you will then know almost half of all the truth about rats and, according to your theories, this will enable you to know the whole truth about human beings.

First construct your maze and then put the rats in it. Observe which way they turn. Some turn one way and some turn the other way. But it begins to look as if rats in general have a tendency to turn towards the left side of the maze. You notice that this left side is the brighter side because it happens to be closer to the window. So you frame in your mind the hypothesis based on your observations: 'Rats turn towards light'. The way you test the hypothesis to see if it is true is by setting up an experiment. That is, you control the conditions.

So you black out the whole laboratory then divide your maze into two sections — one illuminated by an electric bulb, the other completely darkened. Fetch out the rats, put them in the maze and observe carefully what happens in the conditions which you have invented or, as scientists say, standardized. Now, watch the rats for five or six hours and, 'eureka!', they all turn to the light side. The experiment is over and you've won your bet or, more properly, you have validated your hypothesis because what you thought would happen has in fact happened.

Naturally, you wish to bring this important discovery to the attention of the world's press so you decide to repeat the experiment and film it then everyone will be able to see the truth of your hypothesis: 'Rats turn towards the light'. You set up the television camera and prepare to repeat the experiment. But, horror of horrors, the rats begin to turn towards the dark! It looks as if your scientific career is in ruins. Wait a minute. I see why they're running to the dark side. That piece of cheese you were eating has dropped into the dark section of the maze and it is a well-known fact that when it comes to a choice between cheese and light, your average rat will choose the Cheddar every time.

Your hypothesis has not been invalidated after all. What had happened was that something (namely the piece of Cheddar) had interfered with the standard conditions. What you need to do then is simply to frame your new hypothesis about rats more precisely. It won't do to say: 'Rats turn towards the light'. You must say: 'Under standard conditions rats turn towards the light'. And then you will be ready to reveal your momentous scientific discovery to the world. In other words, avoid accidental cheese dropping.

I have deliberately chosen this fairly light-hearted example because it's more fun to write and read about this sort of thing than about 'iron bars floating on water', 'litmus paper turning green' or 'electromagnetometers'. But you should not run away with the idea that scientific method is trivial and just a joke. Usually experiments are important and constructive — testing a new vaccine for example. Or developing a new kind of steel for use in everything from invalid carriages to artificial satellites. The point is the same whichever example we choose whether it's a humorous one about rats or a highly important one about the development of antibiotics. Scientific method always follows the same procedure:

(1) Observation — What is actually going on in a particular environment?
(2) Hypothesis — 'I suspect that so and so is going on.'
(3) Experiment — The arranging of a set of conditions which will tell me if my suspicions are correct. In scientific terms, which will validate my hypothesis. This must be done with absolute care and precision. Any mistake or accident (e.g. falling cheese) will render the experiment useless.
(4) Statement — The summary of results. This is usually called a theory. So we hear of the theory of relativity or the theory of gravitation for instance.

Are Theories Laws?

Sometimes people talk glibly about 'scientific laws' or the 'laws of science' as if these are unalterable things and any speech against them is almost treasonable. The fact is that scientific laws are not unchangeable — quite the reverse. T. H. Huxley wrote of:

> 'The great tragedy of science — the slaying of a beautiful hypothesis by an ugly fact'.

And this is what he meant. We observe, experiment and validate a hypothesis — in physics for example. We issue a theory that atoms are the basic building blocks of matter — the smallest things that there are out of which all other things are made. One day someone comes along and discovers protons and electrons — smaller particles within the atom — and our theory is undermined. This doesn't mean that we must give up science. It does mean that we should frame a better theory — one which, in this case, takes account of the protons and electrons. Science will disappoint us only when we look to it for absolute and eternal certainty. It cannot provide this. What it can give is the best possible account of the way things are at present. There is no telling what tomorrow might bring. Bertrand Russell used to say: 'The chicken which is fed every day eventually gets its neck wrung'.

In this respect scientific theories are like chickens. They persist until something new and unexpected comes along and (I don't mean to be impolite to my chickens) 'changes' them. That is progress in science and not failure. Scientific theories are immensely useful. They tell us what to expect. This is of crucial value if you're designing a boat, a car or an aircraft; or if you're looking for a vaccine or a cure for disease. It tells us what to expect under standard conditions and gives us general rules. But it also tells us to be on the lookout for the unexpected. That it cannot inform us beforehand of the exact nature of the unexpected is not the fault of science. The unexpected belongs to the future and scientific theories are general rules based on past experience; they are not occult predictions about what is to come. We are allowed to expect the sun to rise tomorrow. Indeed we should expect it to rise. But there is the possibility that it might not. Scientists are not crystal gazers.

A good theory is one which accounts for the most number of facts in the least number of words. But no theory can account for *all* the facts simply because we do not know *all* the facts. In physics, Newton's theory seemed for centuries to account for all the facts but in our own period Albert Einstein discovered new facts which caused him to frame a new and improved theory. No doubt one day even Einstein's theory will be superseded.

Those who speak of science as though it were some sort of unalterable and final truth are as bigoted as those who err on the side of irrational dogmatism in religion. Human knowledge is always changing and developing precisely because human beings keep on discovering new facts and having new experiences. Science is a collected body of statements about the world which expresses as accurately as possible the state of our knowledge *now*. It is not a chest full of eternal truths written on tablets of stone; nor is it a computer raised to the level of an all-knowing God. It is extremely valuable and honorable nonetheless.

Science v Religion?

We have talked about religion as in some aspects irrational or non-rational. We have also mentioned the fact that it sometimes seems to attempt to explain the world. Now science is basically rational and it does explain the world. Are science and religion then necessarily in conflict with each other? More controversy, more bitterness, more hot air and more downright nonsense has been spoken and written on the topic of science versus religion than on possibly any other topic known to man.

Thus at the time when Darwin's theory of evolution was new, Bishop Wilberforce made the silly remark to T. H. Huxley that if he (Huxley) was prepared to trace his ancestry back to the monkeys on his father's side, would he be prepared to do the same on his mother's side? Alec Vidler has rightly said that this standard of argument merely reflects the nineteenth century's sentimental attitude towards women and has nothing to do with rational debate at all — let alone with truth.

And some people who believed that the Bible is true word for word claimed that God had put fossils in the rocks deliberately to tempt men and women to the belief that the world was not made in six days. This speaks ill of the ethics of the literalists and even more ill of the ethics of the God in whom they claim to believe! But let us look seriously and without prejudice at the question of whether science and religion contradict each other. Does science 'disprove' the Bible?

Compare these two accounts:

(A)   In six days God made the heaven and the earth and all that is in them. The earth is at the centre. The Sun and the Moon are lights in the sky put there by God for our benefit. The sky is a sort of lid and over the top of the lid is water. God made man out of dust and enlivened him by breathing his Spirit into him. Woman was fashioned out of one of man's ribs. All the animals were made separately as were the plants and all this happened just as God had intended it.

(B)   The universe began thousands of millions of years ago with a big bang and it is expanding into infinite space. Our own planet is a relatively new thing being part of a system of planets which revolve around the Sun. as for the Sun, it is a star like billions of other stars. The earth is not the centre of things. No one knows for certain exactly how life came to be but however, it was a slow process beginning with micro-organisms and developing over millions of years into the species of plant and animal which we now observe. Man is one kind of animal. It is reasonable to suppose that on one or more of the countless billions of planets there is life existing in a far superior form to human life on Earth. Man was not specially created but evolved and there is no reason to think that he is the most highly developed life form in the universe — any more than the fact that he is obviously not the lowest.

The first account is more or less the biblical version — you can find it in the early chapters of Genesis. The second account is a fairly rough and non-technical description of current scientific opinion. Obviously they contradict each other, or do they?

Intentions and Presuppositions

It is a regularly forgotten fact that contradiction can only occur between statements on the same level of discourse. Let me explain by an example. Suppose Jack looks out of the window and says, 'It's raining.' Then Jill looks out and she says 'It's dry.' Now it's obvious that these two statements are contradictory. It is impossible to hold one to be true without denying the other. This is what I mean when I say they are on the same level of discourse.

But imagine Jack looks out and says, 'It's raining cats and dogs" Jill replies, 'No it isn't; it's pouring down.' These two statements cannot possibly be contradictory because they're not on the same level of discourse. Jill's remark is a fairly straightforward, literal description of what's happening. It's raining so hard that it looks as if someone is pouring it down out of the sky. But 'It's raining cats and dogs' isn't meant to be taken literally at all. There are no tumbling wet animals. The statement made by Jack is pictorial or metaphorical. It's an imaginative statement, not a purely descriptive one.

Well then, scientific statements, by the same principle, can only contradict biblical statements if they are on the same level of discourse. They appear to be — they're both of them accounts of the world and how things come to be as they are. Surely they are on the same level and one must therefore be right and the other wrong since each advances different accounts? But in order to be certain that they are on the same level we have to take into consideration the intentions of their writers. What did each wish to convey? And what did each presuppose?

Although the biblical account of creation looks as if it is a catalogue of actual historical facts there is a large body of evidence to indicate that the writer didn't mean us to take what he wrote in an absolutely literal sense. The ancient people who told the biblical creation stories didn't have our modern scientific obsession with the literal descriptive statement. And their presuppositions were different from ours. For instance, they took the fact of God's existence for granted and their intention was to show that all things that have ever occurred have come about through God's will and activity. This is called theocentricity — putting God at the centre of things. It didn't occur to them to doubt God's existence. The Psalmist wrote: 'The *fool* has said in his heart "there is no God".'

What really mattered for the people of the ancient Middle East was that there was a God who was in charge of man's destiny. They presupposed that there was a God and from that presuppositon everything else followed. Is there a world, sun, moon and stars? Then these *must* have been made by God. But the biblical writers were less interested in the actual physical mechanics of *how* God made the world. They were far more interested in what was for them the fact *that* God had made it. They are not at all concerned about historical accuracy and theoretical consistency — for instance there are two accounts of the creation in the early chapters of Genesis and these differ widely! We have seen the same cavalier attitude towards details in the story of the Exodus where, in the space of a dozen verses, there are three or four different versions of the same tale.

Science has quite different intentions and presuppositions. Scientists always seek to answer the question, 'What *exactly* happens?' So when they ask questions about the past, the tense of the verb simply changes: 'What exactly happen*ed*?' This is the intention of science, to discover the literal truth. Furthermore, the scientist doesn't share the biblical writers' presupposition that God exists. This is not to say that scientists are all atheists; many of them do in fact believe in God. But they don't make God into a hypothesis when seeking to explain natural and physical happenings. Instead they try to explain what happens in terms of physical, chemical and mechanical changes and not in terms of supernatural causation.

The main difference between the scientific approach and the biblical one can be illustrated by an example from everyday experience. Suppose someone asks: 'Why is Jane beating Simon over the head with that paddle?'

The scientific answer might well be something like: 'Because the part of her brain which controls aggressive behaviour has ordered the release of adrenalin into her bloodstream etc . . .'

This is the literal answer, the mechanics of what is actually happening. But another answer might be: 'Because he trapped her finger in the boathouse door.'

Both answers are genuine and valid explanations of the same event, they're not contradictory. That's because each answers a different sort of question. The first is a question of mechanics; the second is about purpose. Something like this is true of the relation between Bible stories and scientific accounts.

If you could prove conclusively to one of the ancient biblical writers that the world began with a big bang and that men and women developed through a process of evolution he most probably would not be at all upset. He might find it hard to believe because he is not himself a scientist, but your proof would not cause him to abandon his belief in God. He would simply make God responsible for the big bang or for whatever theory of the earth's origin you happened to favour. The mechanics of how it actually happened wouldn't concern him. It does concern a few religious people (see Chapter 6 on revelation) and it did worry Bishop Wilberforce but that concern is based on a misunderstanding which arises out of a confusion of the intentions and presuppositions of the biblical writers with those of the scientist. The biblical writer didn't believe in a God who simply created the world and then stood back to watch the fun or fell asleep with boredom. For him God, although distinct from the world, was involved in it and in the destiny of his people. If a battle was won or lost, a king proclaimed or a city destroyed it was all according to God's will. God was no philosophical abstraction but a part of living experience. It would no more occur to a biblical writer to doubt God's existence than it would seem reasonable to us to deny the existence of oxygen.

The Climate of Opinion

You might think that's all very well so far. Fair enough, the biblical writers didn't think scientifically so their stories are not rival accounts of how the world is and where it came from. But for the last few hundred years we in the western world have developed scientific methods so that we seek explanations not from the religion of a pre-scientific age but from science itself. And we have found this procedure rewarding. Science does answer our questions in a practical way without bringing in obscure entities like 'God'. More than that, science helps us increasingly not just to understand the world but to change it, to make it more suitable for our habitation. For instance, we have central heating, hot and cold running water, electricity, the irrigation of deserts besides television, telephone and spaceships. What use have we for ancient ideas about God? Surely, that's just a hangover from a primitive age? Although we can't disprove God's existence, we don't need to bring him in to explain things. We can manage very nicely without him. This is the scientific climate of opinion — not interested in philosophical puzzles about whether there is a God or not but practically atheistic in the sense that there is no natural inclination to look for a God as the Explanation of All Things. The practical atheism of the scientific climate of opinion is entertainingly summed up in a modern parable told by Antony Flew in *New Essays in Philosophical Theology:*

> Once upon a time two explorers came upon a clearing in the jungle. In the clearing were growing many flowers and many weeds. One explorer says, 'Some gardener must tend this plot.' The other disagrees, 'There is no gardener.' So they pitch their tents and set a watch. No gardener is ever seen. 'But perhaps he is an invisible gardener.' So they set up a barbed-wire fence. They electrify it. They patrol with bloodhounds. (For they remember how H. G. Well's *The Invisible Man* could be both smelt and touched though he could not be seen.) But no shrieks ever suggested that some intruder has received a shock. No movements of the wire ever betray an invisible climber. The bloodhounds never give cry. Yet the Believer is not convinced. 'But there is a gardener, invisible, intangible, insensible to electric shocks, a gardener who has no scent and makes no sound, a gardener who comes secretly to look after the garden which he loves.' At last the Sceptic despairs, 'But what remains of your original assertion? Just how does what you call an invisible, intangible, eternally elusive gardener differ from an imaginary gardener or even from no gardener at all?'

There it is in a nutshell, in the view of the Sceptical Explorer, the scientific climate of opinion which is practical atheism. God, even if he exists, makes no material difference to anything. Everything can be described without any reference to God at all. So it is as if there is no God.

And if it is always as if there is no God then it is probable that there is in fact no God.

Now I would not number myself among those believers who are against science because they think it contradicts the Bible. No doubt some atheistic scientists would be infuriated at my presumptuousness if I said I believe that science is God-given. So I will not say that either. But I do think that some facts of our experience are probably inexplicable without bringing in the idea of God — and if not literally inexplicable then at least not more plausibly explained by science itself.

Let's have an example. Suppose, as happens not often but sometimes, a man is practically dead, stomach destroyed by cancer. A number of his friends gather together and pray to God for the patient to be healed. In a matter of hours their friend is sitting up in bed, his stomach restored, and asking for something to eat. His recovery is complete and he goes on to live a normal life for a number of years.

A scientist might argue that this 'spontaneous remission', as it is called, is due to natural principles which we do not yet understand but that as science advances we shall gain a greater knowledge of them. After all, this has happened many times in the past when events previously thought to lie under the influence of supernatural causation have turned out to be explainable in ordinary natural terms.

I agree it is at least possible that the scientist is right. I cannot, as I have said, prove the existence of God any more than the scientist can disprove it. But in this case the scientist is merely substituting one unknown — the possible discovery of future scientific principles — for another unknown — the existence of God. And I wonder whether there is not more to it than this. Do we not frequently observe that causes and effects are similar and that usually what we think will happen does happen? We don't walk around with permanently surprised looks on our faces. So might it not be possible that the man near to death recovered because his friend's prayer was answered? Perhaps he would have recovered anyway; maybe not.

But when we look at the thousands of cases of faith healing is it not at least as reasonable to suppose that what happens is a result of prayer, that it is what it seems to be? Science itself operates on the principle of Occam's razor — a principle named after the philosopher William of Occam who recommended that when we are faced with a choice of explanations we should always favour the one which contains the least number of unknowns in it. Is it not then reasonable, on the basis of this very good scientific principle, to believe that sometimes healing comes about in the way that it appears to come about — as a result of a direct prayer for healing? And isn't the 'scientific' answer, which asks us to put our faith in possible principles which we have not yet discovered, a little too vague, too unOccamish? There is no proof of course, but my concern is simply to say that we ought not to be content with the claim that the event I cannot now explain might one day be explained according to a scientific principle which has not yet been discovered. It may all come about as the scientist says but then it may not. In short, God should not be treated as if he was an object of fashion, and just because the current climate of opinion does not readily make room for him we should not regard this as a proof of his non-existence.

A Change of Climate

Recently in science there has been a drift away from the materialistic and mechanistic point of view which regards the universe as if it were a machine. As I say, we should beware of taking too much notice of fashions but it is a fact that the 'mechanical universe' has only been the orthodox scientific view for about two to three hundred years or so. In our own century, scientists seem to be returning to a doctrine that was held in the so-called 'pre-scientific' era — a doctrine which states that the universe is more like mind stuff than matter stuff. As we saw in the chapter on 'God', this change of emphasis, change of climate if you wish, is coming about through research into particle physics. The basic building blocks of the universe are turning out not to be solid blocks after all but things that are more like impulses or even ideas. An interesting question: 'Who's ideas?'

And while we should continue to value science for all the knowledge and benefits it brings we should also remember that there is another way of talking about the universe besides the language of scientific method. And that's the language of poetry and religious and spiritual expression — the language in which we try to capture and describe those strange feelings of awe and wonder I talked about at the beginning of this chapter. When astrophysicists have taken a rest from baffling us with 'light years', 'pulsars', 'quasars' and 'parsecs' there is still the vision of the night sky. Why does it move us to wonder, to astonishment, and finally, perhaps, to silence?

I'm not claiming any ultimate answers. Only that it all seems so complex, so beautiful and sometimes so cruel and horrible that I cannot make sense of the universe without talking about pattern and purpose. I suppose it's possible that everything happened by chance, by cosmic accident and fluke mutation but as science itself uncovers more and more wonders I come to think with Francis Bacon that 'this universal frame' has a mind. The philosopher Wittgenstein puts it well: 'It's not *how* the world is that's mystical, It's *that* it is.'

Just sit back and wonder 'Why is there anything at all?' You won't prove the existence of God, nor disprove it but what do you think? And what do you feel?

Exercise
(1) Look at the five definitions of 'religion'. Invent five sentences using each definition in turn. Can you think of a sixth definition?
(2) What is the difference between a belief and an attitude?

(3) Is 'feeling religious' an argument for the existence of God?

(4) Where do our feelings of awe and wonder come from?

(5) Why are films like The Exorcist *and* Dracula *so popular in an age of scientific explanation?*

(6) Do people see ghosts because they eat cheese?

(7) Describe what is involved in working from:

  (a) observation;   *(c) experiment;*

  (b) hypothesis;   *(d) theory.*

(8) What are 'standard conditions' and why are they important in science?

(9) Does science give us any certain knowledge?

(10) Why are scientific theories like chickens?

(11) What is the difference between the biblical account of creation and a scientific theory about the origin of the universe? Do they contradict each other?

(12) What is the difference between an invisible, intangible gardener and no gardener at all?

(13) Is it more reasonable to believe that everything has come about through chance or that the universe is directed by the mind of God?

(14) Explain the principle of Occam's razor.

(15) What do you think Wittgenstein meant when he said, 'It's that the world is that's mystical'?

(16) Why is there anything at all?

(17) If everything comes by chance then our reason comes by chance, then there is no reason for reason in the first place — is there?

5 God and Evil

The puzzles surrounding the use of the words 'good' and 'evil' are numerous. Complete books have been written in the attempt to find out what they mean. Here are a few illustrations of some of the problems — I'll deal only with 'good' because the same difficulties apply to 'evil' only, as it were, the other way round.

First then, is 'good' the name of a quality possessed by some objects and not by others? We talk of a good cricket bat, a good summer etc. Well if it is such a quality we can't detect it in the way we normally detect qualities such as 'hardness', 'strength' or 'yellowness'. Secondly, how can we apply the same word 'good' to different kinds of things and be clear what we are saying? I mean the goodness of a cricket bat is something quite different from the goodness of a good summer. How then can I use the same word?

Thirdly, if I think something is good and you think it's awful how do we decide who's right? Does this mean that 'good' is just a word to describe personal preferences and prejudices? These are just three of the difficulties in saying what we mean by 'good'. For a more complete discussion of the problem, but one that is straightforward, refer to Chapter 9 of my book *Beginning Philosophy*.

When we use the words 'good' and 'evil' in this chapter we shall be thinking generally of their common everyday meaning. That is, good things are to be regarded as those which are obviously pleasant and beneficial and evil things are those which are unpleasant and harmful. I'm afraid we shall be talking about evil for most of the time because it is the existence of evil which has proved to be such a mighty problem for those who believe that the universe is the creation of a good God.

Usually when theologians talk about evil they mean pain and suffering endured by man. They often include so called 'natural' evils in this category — harmful and destructive events such as earthquakes and floods. So for our purposes here we can do as C. S. Lewis did in *The Problem of Pain* and talk about evil in terms of pain, suffering and apparent purposelessness.

The problem hinted at in the title of this chapter then is of how to reconcile belief in a good and all-powerful God with the fact of suffering in the world. Let's be clear from the start, evil is a problem for the believer and not for the non-believer. I don't mean to suggest that the non-believer doesn't have his pains and troubles to the same degree as the believer — of course he does. But he is not faced with the added problem of squaring these unpleasantnesses with the existence of a good God, precisely because he doesn't believe in God at all. For the non-believer the universe isn't under the control of a guiding moral purpose. Events simply occur according to the normal process of the world, the workings of morally neutral 'nature'. As one philosopher put it, 'For the non-believer it's just one damned thing after another'.

And I don't want anyone to run away with the idea that I believe you can't be good without a belief in God. Many atheists and humanists have led lives of such goodness and unselfishness that they are an example to us all — and to some Christians in particular. What I am saying is that if atheists don't have the comfort of belief (if belief is a comfort) they don't have the problems connected with it either. Mainly they don't have to deal with the fact (if it is a fact) that a supposedly good God allows evil and suffering in the world. Non-believers no doubt have other problems such as 'Where did the world come from?' 'Why is there order and pattern in creation?' and 'Where do we get our idea of goodness from if God does not exist?' Presumably, they have worked out answers to these questions — answers which do not involve them in having to affirm the existence of God. Our problem is simply stated if not easily solved: 'How is it that an all-powerful God, who is also completely good, allows pain and suffering in the world?'

Is it all Our Fault?

Some argue that suffering is a consequence of sin, of disobedience to the will of God. God did not intend evil and suffering in his world but man is prone to disobedience and suffering is a consequence of that disobedience. It is said that God made certain laws to govern conduct in his world. If these laws are kept or respected then good will follow; if they are ignored then only evil ensues. Furthermore, God does not compel obedience by his mighty power but gives man freedom to choose. The writer of Genesis puts this doctrine pictorially in chapter three of his book. He imagines that when the first man and the first woman were made, God put them in a delightful garden — the Garden of Eden. He allowed them to eat of the fruit of any tree they wished but from the tree of knowledge of good and evil they must not eat. But the serpent tempted the woman and the woman encouraged the man and they ate of the fruit of the tree of knowledge and so disobeyed God. Therefore God cast them out of the garden because of their disobedience. So by man came evil.

This is a story, a kind of parable or myth. It's not literally true but it gives a pictorial account of the belief that God created everything good, and evil is purely and simply the result of man's disobedience to God's will. Suppose we forget the actual words of this interesting story for a moment and concentrate on what it is trying to tell us. It's saying that God intends us to live a perfect existence but we always spoil his plans by choosing to disobey him. Presumably God could have so arranged things that we always as a matter of fact choose to obey him. But then, it is argued, we would not be human beings at all — more like machines or robots. And God will not overrule our freedom of choice because that would be to deny our humanity — to treat us as less than human. C. S. Lewis gives us an example in *The Problem of Pain*:

> We can, perhaps, conceive of a world in which God corrected the results of this abuse of free-will by His creatures at every moment: so that a wooden beam became soft as grass when it was used as a weapon, and the air refused to obey me if I attempted to set up in it the sound waves that carry lies or insults. But such a world would be one in which wrong actions were impossible, and in which, therefore, freedom of the will would be void . . . Try to exclude the possibilty of suffering which the order of nature and the existence of free-wills involve, and you find you have excluded life itself.

Many believers find this is a satisfactory explanation of the problem of evil and suffering — it comes about through man's disobedience. Others are less than satisfied. They argue as follows.

First, if God is all-powerful then he would have known from the very beginning, before man had been created, what the result would be — that there would be disobedience and consequent suffering. Therefore it would have been better not to have created anything in the first place. For a God who did not know what was going to happen would not be all-powerful; a God who did know but who proceeded to create cannot be regarded as perfectly good. So 'God' is either weak or immoral; in both cases he is not the being whom believers describe as 'the Almighty God'.

Secondly, not all evil is the result of disobedience. It may be that wars and fighting are the result of man's selfish and sinful intent and that he has only himself to blame for the damage he does through the exercise of his aggressive and warlike lusts. But what about earthquakes? What about floods, lightnings, storms and falling meteorites? It is difficult to see that these are in any way connected with human behaviour or morality. It's not your own fault, is it, if the ground under your feet begins to shake and to crack and the houses fall down?

So even if the argument that certain evils are necessary as a consequence of man's freewill is held to be convincing, the believer still has to account for natural disasters. It looks as if God has created a faulty and imperfect world. Surely an all-powerful God could do better than that?

Excessive Suffering

Even if we were to admit that some small amount of suffering was an unavoidable consequence of creation (and we do not necessarily accept this doctrine) how is it that there is so much pain and suffering? Schopenhauer put it nicely:

> A quick test of the question that enjoyment outweighs pain in this world, or that they are at any rate balanced, would be to compare the feelings of an animal engaged in eating another with those of the animal being eaten.

Wars, murders and famines seem to be the general rule. Half of the world is underfed. Man's instinct is to have children and the result is that he is breeding his family into starvation. Every time you switch on the radio or the television you hear reports of the latest disagreements and strife. And there is sickness and untimely death. Children sometimes die and their parents are heartbroken. Fathers die and leave the family bereft. All the time we have the added agony of the knowledge that we ourselves will one day die. As Shakespeare says:

> Golden lads and girls all must,
> As chimney-sweepers, come to dust.

Surely an all-powerful God could have created a better world than this one! We can imagine that a creator who was not all-powerful, but a fairly powerful spirit who was also a good craftsman, could have done better. But this world, if it had a creator at all, must have been made by a bungler or a sadist.

One answer to this charge is that we do not live in an ideal world, for an ideal world is not possible. We do live in the best of all possible worlds. A world in which certain evils are necessary in order for certain goods to exist. For example, if there was no war, there would not be the chance for men and women to show the higher virtues of courage and self-sacrifice. Without hunger there would be no satisfaction in eating. This argument may have a measure of academic persuasion (though even that is doubtful) to a college professor theorizing quietly to himself in his warm and comfortable study in the beautiful and ancient city of Oxford. But it sounds like a sick joke to a crippled and starving refugee from, say, a bloody civil war in Africa. Wouldn't this seem to him not the best but the worst of all possible worlds?

Is it the Devil's Fault?

Another attempt to answer the problem of evil in the world involves the Devil. He is supposed to be a spiritual power, something like God only wicked instead of good. Some religions picture the world as a kind of theatre of war where the Devil and God engage each other in conflict using men and women as their 'soldiers'. Christianity sometimes appears to take this view in such hymns as *Stand up for Jesus, ye soldiers of the cross* where individual Christians are regarded as combatants in the heavenly divisions. *Like a mighty army moves the church of God, Fight the Good*

Fight and *Soldiers of Christ Arise* are further examples of the spiritual
battle theory of good versus evil.

All the same, this solution is not without its difficulties. First the
existence of the Devil is itself problematical. How do we know he exists?
Because we feel tempted, perhaps. But the temptation may be nothing
other than inner tensions and stresses caused by a conflict of desires.
Which is easier to understand 'The Devil has a gold watch' or simply 'I'd
really rather like to have that gold watch.' The problem of evil is, as I said
at the start of this chapter, a problem for believers. And that is because it
challenges the rationality of belief in God. God is defined as a supernatural
being of almighty power and total goodness. But we cannot prove that
such a power exists in fact. So does it not simply multiply our confusion
to claim that there is another spiritual force in the universe, only this time
it's a bad one? We seem to be in danger of bringing in the Devil to get God
off the hook. Those who do algebra know that the most difficult equations
are the ones which contain the greatest number of unknowns. Is it really
any help to suggest the existence of a further invisible supernatural power
as an assistance when our belief in the first invisible and supernatural
power is under threat? Aren't we much more sensible if we prefer Occam's
razor? After all, we've enough problems trying to defend the belief in one
supernatural power let alone two of them.

Secondly, what (if he or she exists) is the status of the Devil? Is he like
God in power and form but evil instead of good? In other words, are we to
think of him as God's equal? If so, then we have even more trouble for we
are suggesting the existence of two gods. Once we make this step there
seems no good reason to stop. If two gods, why not three, or four, or four
thousand? Hindus believe in many gods but then they have a different
concept of God and the relation of God to the world which we shall look
at later in the chapter. But the Jewish and Christian traditions on which
western civilization is based know of only one God. Everything is created
by him, even the Devil.

In the Old Testament there's a marvellous story about a man called Job.
It's an attempt to answer the problem of evil. At the beginning of the
book it says:

> Now there was a day when the sons of God came to present them-
> selves before the Lord, and Satan came also among them.

Satan is just another name for the Devil. So the Old Testament sees the
Devil as one of God's sons, that is as someone created by God. If the Devil
(a force for evil) was created by God, doesn't that make God responsible
for the creation of evil? Some have argued that the Devil was, like man,
created good but that he turned away from God in an act of disobedience
before the world was made. If that is so, then the same arguments which
apply as criticisms of the 'freewill defence' in connection with man also
apply in the 'freewill defence' in connection with the Devil. Moreover, if

God is all-powerful, he would have known in advance that the Devil, once created, would one day turn against him. And he would know therefore of the suffering which would ensue. So it would have been better — assuming that God is all good — not to have created anything. At the very least one might say rather irreverently, that God, having seen what happened in the case of the Devil, ought not to have gone on to create man and thus make the same mistake twice over!

It may be that there is a Devil but I have tried to show that his existence does not account for the origin of evil, nor does it take away from God (if he exists) any of his responsibility for his creation.

Are These Things Sent to Try Us?

It is sometimes argued that evil exists in order to test our faith. Perhaps this is a solution to the puzzle about pain, suffering and a God of love. Maybe God knows that it is very important — ultimately important — for us to have faith in him come what may and the evil is the come what may. It is suggested that human beings, lovers and friends, sometimes test one another's love and faithfulness. 'If we part for six months, that will cause suffering, but at the end of that time if we've remained faithful we'll enjoy a much deeper relationship.' Such words a young lady might write to her young man having read some advice from one of the agony columnists.

Perhaps then, this is how it is with God. The pain and suffering of this world is a time of testing and if we remain faithful to him he will reward us with everlasting happiness in heaven. The difficulty with this approach lies in our understanding of the nature of God (if he exists) as communicated to us by the highest aspects of our religious tradition. It's all very well for imperfect men and women, boys and girls, to test one another in this way but God is *not* an imperfect human being — he is almighty and completely good. It is impossible to imagine that a perfect being, God, would make his creatures suffer so terribly in order to test their faith. Does the God of love use the earthquake and the famine to test the strength of religious conviction of a child who cannot yet read?

Besides there's something odd about the whole notion of such a test. If God is almighty then he knows the outcome before the experiment takes place. What need therefore for the test? In any case the whole idea of a test involves the possibility of pass and fail. If nobody fails then, as I've already said, what is the use of such a test to the all-knowing God? If, on the other hand, (as usually happens in tests and examinations) some people fail, what does God do with the failures? Are we to suppose that the almighty and ever-loving God adds yet more punishment to what they've suffered already?

Will it all be All Right in the End?

Another argument goes by the fancy name of 'eschatological justification'.

'Eschatology' is a word derived from the Greek and it means simply 'about the end'. So, in other words, eschatological justification says: 'Don't worry. It will be all right in the end'. Professor Hick believes this and you can read his development of the argument which he wrote in a famous book *Evil and the God of Love*. I once heard Professor Hick defending his point of view in a television interview. He said that life is like a train journey and we are all still on this journey which is not completed until death. Naturally some parts of the journey are more comfortable than others but the judgement as to whether it is a good journey cannot be made until it is over — until it can be viewed as a whole.

According to Professor Hick when we die we shall meet God and then we shall know the purpose of suffering. We shall see that the journey was worth it. I could not bring myself to feel very impressed by this doctrine because it looked, and still looks, to me as if Professor Hick is affirming what is at issue in order to prove his point and therefore arguing in a circle. Let me explain what I mean by 'affirming the issue'.

The fact of evil is in itself an argument against the existence of a good God. It will not do therefore to state, as if it were a counter to that argument, that the answer will be revealed by God himself in the end. For it is the very existence of God which is in doubt. It's like waiting for a cat to come home in order to find out if you ever had a cat in the first place!

It doesn't look as if we can solve the problem of evil by rational argument because there seems to be no denying the logic of the statement that if God is responsible for everything then, even if indirectly, he is responsible for evil. If God exists and is all-powerful, then he knew that evil would be a consequence of creation. why, then, did he make anything in the first place, knowing as he must have done, that pain and suffering would ensue? Perhaps there is no God and the non-believer is right that 'It's just one damned thing after another.' The Christian believes that there is a God and there is purpose in the world. And God isn't indifferent to evil and suffering but he has done and is continuing to do something about it. This belief is usually expressed in what are called theories of atonement. We shall have a look at some of them now.

A Ransom Paid to the Devil?

Since evil and suffering came by man's disobedience and therefore by his separation from God then, according to the Christian belief, the first need is for that rift between man and God to be healed. This healing, this act of putting right what has gone wrong is called atonement. If we break the word up we can see its meaning clearly — 'at, one, ment'. Man cannot do this because of his disobedient nature so, if anything is to be done at all, it must be the action of God.

Christians believe that God worked atonement, that he put right what had gone wrong, by the life, death and resurrection of Jesus Christ. They claim that Jesus of Nazareth was no ordinary man but the Son of God, or God become man. This actual historical act of God becoming man is what Christians celebrate at Christmas. And the story of Jesus' life and all that happened to him is God's action in this world to put things right, to overcome evil, to bring men back to a full relationship with him.

There are difficulties attached to this belief as is shown by the fact that there isn't just one theory of the atonement but many. Christians all agree that 'God was in Christ reconciling the world to himself' — as the New Testament says he was — but they disagree about the way this actually happened.

One of the earliest theories of atonement speaks in terms of God paying a ransom to the Devil. It pictures men and women as hostages of the Devil since they gave in to his temptation. We are all in the power of Satan and cannot of ourselves do anything about our position. But God can. And what he did was to trick the Devil. He sent his Son into the world in the person of Jesus Christ and allowed him to be captured by the Devil. This is what happened at the crucifixion. But the trick was that God, being more powerful than the Devil, could not be held by him — nor could his son, Jesus Christ. Jesus rose from the dead and freed men from the Devil's hold. By his death he effected the ransom and by rising to life again he defeated the powers of evil.

These are images and pictures of course and Christians would insist that we do not take them so literally as to believe in a pantomime Devil with pitchfork and tail. Nevertheless, most Christians do believe in a power of evil which we may as well call 'the Devil' and that Jesus did in fact rise from the dead. But one of the problems about this particular theory, and indeed about all theories of the atonement, is that it asks us to accept a lot of other events as true in order for the theory to work. None of these events can be proved to have happened — the resurrection of Jesus from the dead for instance. And besides this criticism there is another very important objection. It is the problem of interpretation. For argument's sake let us assume that certain facts are not in dispute. Let us suppose that Jesus was born about two thousand years ago, that he lived his life in Palestine, that he was put to death by the Jewish authorities and the Romans and that he rose from the dead. This, even if we accept it all as literal truth, does not prove that Jesus died for our sakes or that he rose from the dead in order to vanquish the powers of darkness. All we are strictly entitled to say, even if we believe the whole biblical account of the life, death and resurrection of Jesus, is that it happened. The reasons for its happening are a matter of interpretation.

Take an example from daily living as an illustration of what I mean about this. War is, unfortunately, a common enough occurrence. Suppose a soldier is shot dead. The parson might preach at his funeral about how the soldier was a true patriot and died for the love of his country. That may be true, of course. But for someone looking on from a distance (one is tempted to say, 'Especially if that distance was one of two thousand years') all that is immediately obvious is that a soldier has died. He may have been shot by accident. Perhaps he was no patriot but joined the army because he was forced. I am saying that no event is susceptible to only one interpretation. The event itself cannot be its own interpretation. It is for others who come after to evaluate the event and describe its meaning. So it may be true that Jesus lived, died, suffered and rose again, but the conclusion that he did all this 'for us men and for our salvation' is an interpretation. Christians admit this and say it is a matter of faith. As we know faith can be misplaced. I'm not saying that the Christian interpretation of these events in the life of Jesus is false or unjustified, only that it is just one interpretation and there are others. For instance, that Jesus was regarded as a dangerous rebel by the Roman Garrison in Judea and so they had him put to death. Even if he really rose from the dead and appeared to his disciples that would not prove he did it for our sakes. There is even a remote possibility that resurrection is a natural phenomenon, though one so rare that it happens say, only once in every ten thousand years.

When we look at the ransom theory in more detail we find other objections to it. First of all its doubtful morality. Would an almighty and perfect God stoop to such a low trick as deliberately to deceive the Devil? Also, even supposing there really is a Devil, would a being of his supernatural power and cunning fall for such a simple trick? The ransom theory is often pictured as God fishing to catch the Devil with Christ as the bait. You might think that Satan, who was perceptive enough to find a way of spoiling God's plans in the first place, would have seen the hook.

Atonement by Example

We are all at some time in our lives encouraged to follow good examples. Train like the world-class athletes and you'll win the prize. Follow the example of pay restraint shown by the engineers and we'll all be rich. Study like your sister and you too will get to the university. Well the example, or 'exemplerance theory' as it is sometimes called, urges us to look at Christ's action as an example of perfect obedience of God and then, so it is alleged, we shall be moved to turn to God ourselves.

Those who uphold the example theory often quote the words of St Paul in his letter to the Church at Rome:

> You could hardly bring yourself to die for a *just* man, though you might be brave enough to die for a *good* man. But God loves us so much that Christ died for us even though we are *sinners*.

The great advantage of this theory is that it doesn't ask us to accept quaint stories about God making deals with the Devil only to win them by greater power or trickery. It says simply: God knows that evil and suffering exist in the world and that the source of all this is man's disobedience.

But he knows that the answer to (or the cure for) our disobedience is love that is so strong it will suffer even death for the beloved. So God is showing us in the death of Jesus that he loves us. This great demonstration of his love for us is what should make us turn to God and love him — because he first loved us. And if we love God then we are at peace.

The trouble with the example theory is, unfortunately, that it just doesn't work. Some people have turned to God as a result of Jesus' example but millions know the story of the crucifixion and either don't believe it or at least don't let it change their attitude towards God. And in any case, quite apart from the inward good it may do to the hearts of men and women as individuals, the example of Christ hasn't done anything about the amount of actual suffering in the world. If anything, this has increased. We can think of the crusades and scores of other wars fought in Christ's name; all the old evils of suffering and starvation are still with us; Christianity itself has merely added to the sum of religious prejudice and bigotry.

Perhaps this is an exaggeration. Those who believe the exemplerance theory can point to many individuals who down the ages have turned to God through hearing the gospel. And they have lived beautiful lives of love and self-sacrifice. What about the saints? 'Lights of the world in their several generations' as it says in the prayer. But no one can deny that to the realistic observer it does not appear that Christianity has on balance affected the total of human misery at all significantly one way or the other.

Penal Substitution

This doctrine states that because of his disobedience man deserves to be condemned and punished by God. 'Penal' is a word connected with the word 'punishment'. We talk about prisons and 'penal institutions' and of 'paying the penalty' for our misdemeanours. Well, the theory of penal substitution says that God punished his son Jesus Christ in our place. What we need to do is simply to believe this and turn to God then all will be well.

The same objection — that it doesn't seem to have worked — that we applied to the exemplerance theory can, of course, also be applied to the doctrine of penal substitution. Men's hearts still incline to evil and there is an excess of suffering in the world. In the same way, anyone defending the theory can always say that it has worked in some cases and then, adopting Professor Hick's eschatological justification, add that it will be seen to have worked entirely in the end.

There are other objections. First, how can it be possible that one man, even if he was the Son of God, could bear the punishment due to the whole world? No doubt crucifixion is an extremely painful death, but can a few hours of even the most terrible pain balance or cancel out all the world's evils from the beginning until the end — if there is to be an end?

Secondly, isn't there something downright immoral and unjust in punishing someone for what is really the fault of other people? God's son is regarded by Christians as without sin, wholly good and devoted to his Father in Heaven. It seems impossible that this Father in Heaven, the almighty and perfect God, should commit an act of such monstrous injustice as to punish the innocent for the sake of the guilty.

But Christians will argue that he did this because he really loves us. Very well then, if he really loves us why doesn't he simply forgive us, wipe the slate clean, clear up the mess? Those who uphold penal substitution will reply that while God is a God of love he is also a God of justice. And so he cannot simply pretend that sin and disobedience never happened; it must be atoned for. By giving his Son to die for us God both demonstrates his love and satisfies his justice at the same time.

I think there's a contradiction here in that love and justice are incompatible. Love goes far beyond justice. It is a much higher moral concept. Justice cries 'fair do's' and 'an eye for an eye; a tooth for a tooth'; 'give me six of one and I'll give you half a dozen of the other'. Love forgives, cancels debts, surpasses the accountancy of justice. As St Paul says:

> Love is longsuffering and kind. It is not envious. It is not easily provoked and thinks no evil . . . Love endures all things . . .

The theory of penal substitution conjures up the picture of God as a heavenly cashier or accountant dealing in sins and moral judgements as if they were cash. If one pile is too high, he'll move a few moral cheques across to see that things balance. this strikes me as being more like the ethics of Scrooge than love of a Heavenly Father for his children.

Summary

In short, I don't think that any of the answers mentioned in this chapter are solutions to the problem of evil and suffering. We are bound to come back in the end to the undeniable logic of the statement that, if God made everything and in his own almighty way is responsible for it, in some way or other, direct or indirect, he is also responsible for the evil in the world. The only other conclusion is, I believe, that there is no God. I shall say no more about this now and leave what follows from this opinion until the last chapter where I hope it will be seen to tie up with other equally difficult problems raised all through this book.

Exercises
(1) Is there good and evil in the world? Or are there just events and do we invent the words 'good' and 'evil' for convenience?
(2) Do the words 'good' and 'evil' mean the same as the words 'pleasure' and 'pain'?
(3) Is an earthquake an evil, or is it simply a natural event — neither good nor evil?

(4) *Why is evil a problem for those who believe in God?*

(5) *If God is all-powerful and all-good where does evil come from?*

(6) *Is evil all our fault? Is some of it our fault?*

(7) *Is there anything we can do about evil?*

(8) *What has evil to do with freedom of the will? Tell a story to explain your answer.*

(9) *Do we feel pain more intensely than we feel pleasure?*

(10)Is this the 'best of all possible worlds'?

(11)Do you believe in the Devil?

(12)Is there a power of evil, or is what we call evil simply an absence of good?

(13)Could it be that evil things are 'sent to try us'?

(14)Is the doctrine of eschatological justification believable? Will it 'all be alright in the end'?

(15)Arrange a class debate on one of the theories of atonement.

6 Revelation

In all the earlier chapters we have been arguing 'upwards', as it were, to God. Is there any evidence to support the view that there is a corresponding 'downward' movement to us from God? In other words, has God revealed anything about himself to us directly? Our first approach to the question of God's existence was based on our own human ability to reason things out for ourselves — that is to start with man and try and work towards the truth about God (if he exists). Those who believe in revelation argue that God has communicated to us the fact of his existence and something of his nature in a direct way. What are we to make of this argument?

Some say that we could not have thought of God at all unless God himself planted the idea of his existence in our minds. These argue that natural theology — using the reason to try and arrive at the truth about God — is either a complete waste of time or that it is only possible because of God's original revelation of himself. We have to ask, if God is alleged to have revealed himself to us, what form this revelation has taken.

But first we must ask why, given revelation, God has not revealed himself to everyone. Those who believe in revelation have a variety of answers to this question. First, they say that God chooses only a few witnesses to his existence and it is not up to us to question his way of working. God reveals himself to whom he will. God is God. We are only human. It is not for us to tell God his business.

Secondly, it may be argued that God does in fact reveal himself to everyone but most people are so blind or careless that they ignore the revelation. We might call this the 'keep off the grass' theory of revelation. I mean, we all know that there are signs warning us to keep off the grass but sometimes we're so busy rushing about that we fail to see the notice, or else we see it but ignore it because it's quicker to walk over the grass than it is to walk all the way round the path. So with God. According to this theory he reveals himself to all people but not all people notice the revelation. In order to see, it is necessary to open one's eyes.

Thirdly, it is suggested that God's revelation of himself is a subtle thing. It is not blinding and compelling like a thunderstorm for that would force us to believe. And force would overrule our freewill. God always respects our freewill and so he will not reveal himself in a way which gives us no choice about whether to believe in him or not. Room must be left for faith.

Let's take the first answer: God chooses only a few witnesses and it is

not up to us to question his way of working. We might reasonably object
to this that it is an unfair method of procedure — especially for a God who, if
the Ten Commandments are anything to go by, has such a strong interest
in justice. Here we are puzzling and suffering before the mighty problem
of whether there is a God or not; whether we are beings who possess
immortal souls; whether our final destiny is not to be left to rot in the
graveyard but to live with God forever in heaven. Here we are puzzled,
anxious and afraid. It's not much comfort to us to be told: 'Don't worry,
I know God hasn't revealed himself to you, but he has revealed himself to
Sonia and Martin in the next street.' This doesn't seem a just or fair thing
to do.

Then what about the 'keep off the grass' theory? It says: God reveals
himself to us all but not all of us notice his revelation. Perhaps we might
reply, 'Well I can understand overlooking a keep off the grass notice but
how could I possibly miss a revelation of God? He is the Supreme Being,
all powerful, all good. Surely I couldn't help noticing him if he really had
revealed himself to me!'

Finally, there's the doctrine that God's revelation is a subtle thing and
leaves room for faith. This seems to be a very strange argument. For if
God's revelation is so subtle (weak even?) as to leave room for us to doubt
it, in what sense is it a revelation at all? If I ask you to believe that there
are ten toffees in the toffee tin without opening the tin, there is room for
doubt or faith. You can believe what I say or not as you choose. But if I
open the tin and reveal the ten toffees then there is an end of all doubt —
the existence of the toffees is beyond dispute. In short, this objection is
based on the way we use the words 'revelation' and 'reveal'. We use them
in order to put an end to doubt and speculation once and for all. Any
supposed revelation which leaves room for doubt is not really a revelation
at all.

Which God Reveals?

Let us suppose that God does reveal himself to us. Unfortunately this still
doesn't clear up the problem for us. It is not just Christians who claim to
know God through revelation but Muslims, Hindus and Jews. And since all
these faiths present different ideas, pictures and doctrines of God, how are
we to tell which is the true revelation and which are false? Take a specific
example: Muslims and Jews believe that God is one; that he is single and
indivisible. Christians also believe that there is one God but that he has
revealed himself as Father, Son and Holy Spirit — three Persons in one
God. Which doctrine is true? Or are they all false?

Sometimes Christians argue for the doctrine of progressive revelation —
that God reveals something of himself to begin with and then, as man
becomes ready, he reveals more. So they say that God revealed himself in
part to the Jews of the Old Testament period but that he increased that

revelation through the coming of his Son Jesus Christ in the New Testament. Naturally, this is regarded as an insult by many Jews because they do not accept the teaching of the New Testament at all and resent having their religion unfavourably compared with Christianity.

Some say that the 'Gods' of all the main religions of the world are partial revelations of the One True God — that the One True God reveals himself in different ways on different occasions to different people. Once more, the problem with this interpretation is easily seen when we ask the question, 'In what sense can these various, and at times contradictory, revelations really be called revelations?' When we use the word 'revelation' we speak of something plainly shown. How can a logical contradiction be the nature of something plainly shown? God cannot be at the same time One Person (Islam and Judaism) and Three Persons (Christianity).

Is Revelation Possible?

Of course, if there really is an almighty God then he can do exactly what he wishes and if he chooses to reveal himself to mortal man, then reveal himself he will and there's an end of the problem. Apart from the fact that we could often wish God's revelations of himself were a little clearer and more definite, the question arises whether it is ever possible to recognize a revelation when we're supposed to have been given it.

We've all heard tales of desert explorers who think that they have suddenly come upon an oasis just as they are on the very point of passing out through thirst. Then they discover to their distress that it wasn't an oasis at all — only a mirage. How do we know that what we take to be a revelation of God isn't something like a mirage — an illusion or a delusion? Mirages are common occurrences. We've all seen what we've taken to be pools of water on the road ahead only to find that these 'evaporate' as soon as the car we're travelling in comes to where they are supposed to be. We can all make pictures in the fire and in the clouds. What guarantee do we have that what we take to be a revelation of God isn't after all merely an instance of overactive imagination?

More than this, how do we know that what we call 'a revelation' might be nothing but a natural phenomenon? We've noticed already that this was one possible explanation of miracles. And at one time men would have regarded an eclipse of the sun or a flash of lightning as examples of divine revelations. Nowadays we can explain these in purely natural terms. Perhaps present-day 'revelations' will soon be dismissed in similar terms?

In any case, suppose you yourself had been fortunate enough to experience a direct revelation of God. How would you know it was a genuine revelation and not a delusion? Also, how would you go about persuading anyone else that you had in fact been given a revelation by God himself. The fact that you would be laughed at is no evidence against your claim. They laughed at Copernicus when he told them the earth is round. But what language could you use to convince your audience without giving the impression that you'd gone bonkers? Someone once said: 'If you say you talk to God, they'll respect you for that. That's prayer. But if you say God talks to you, they'll put you away. That's lunacy.'

In fact most of us would not claim to have had a direct revelation of God himself. We might be prepared to say that at times we felt sure of his presence but then the feeling of certainty went away. So we are usually dependent on second-hand information for our knowledge of God — that is on the revelation which someone else is supposed to have had. Some people say that there is a permanent record of God's revelation in the words of the Bible. Let us examine this doctrine and see whether we can discover if it is true or false.

Biblical Revelation — The Narrow Approach

Every religion has its holy book so we are faced with the problem of choosing between holy books since each one is different, and says different things about God. This is the same difficulty we met at the start of this chapter when we were trying to choose between revelations of the 'true God' according to alternative religions. We saw that there is no easy answer to that problem. But let us suppose that facts had been otherwise. Let us suppose that the Christian Bible — the books of the Old and New Testaments — is the true revelation of God and that the others don't count. This is only an exercise on my part to narrow the field. I don't believe that the holy books of other religions are worthless. On the contrary I think we can learn a lot about God from the Hindu Scriptures and the Koran as well as from the Bible. But that's a personal opinion. For the sake of argument let us imagine that the Bible is the one holy book which is a revelation of God himself.

As you come to the fifth and sixth forms and think about making your way in the world you will come across people who will tell you that the Bible is true literally, word for word. If you go to college or university you will come across such people sooner rather than later. They may describe themselves as Evangelical Christians or simply as Christians. They might possibly belong to a Christian society in the college and perhaps they will ask you along to one of their meetings. Not all young people who are Christians, and by no means all Christians at universities, believe that the Bible is true word for word. But often those who do hold that doctrine are the most vocal representatives you are likely to meet. Now so far in this book we have not been able to prove any doctrine — that is to establish it beyond doubt. I am happy therefore to tell you that we can prove that the doctrine that the Bible is true word for word is quite definitely false. And we can prove it beyond all doubt and in a way which is so easy to understand that it lies beyond the grasp of nobody's mind. Proof is a rare event, so let's get on with it.

In a book called *Fundamentalism* (those who believe the Bible to be true word for word are sometimes called 'fundamentalists') James Barr produced the following table which compared different biblical acounts of the same historical events:

	Samuel/Kings account	*Chronicles account*
Taken by David	II Samuel 8:4 1700 horsemen 20 000 footmen	I Chronicles 18:4 1000 chariots 7000 horsemen 20 000 footmen
Mercenaries of Ammonites	II Samuel 10:6 20 000 footmen 1000 + 12 000 men	I Chronicles 19:7 32 000 chariots and the army of king of Maacah
Slain by David	II Samuel 10:18 700 charioteers 40 000 horsemen	I Chronicles 19:18 7000 charioteers 40 000 horsemen

There is more to this table but I will not quote it in full for fear of boring you with historical detail. But you see the point? If two different parts of the Bible describe the same event differently in points of detail so that they contradict each other, then one of them (at least) must be wrong. Therefore, the Bible cannot all be true word for word.

The reason I am making such a meal out of this is not just because I'm overjoyed at coming upon the rare event of proof but because logical contradictions are nonsense and nonsense should always be exposed for what it is. Particularly when that nonsense attaches itself to such an important issue as the truth of religion based on the existence of God. I have confessed to the reader that as a matter of fact I personally believe there is a God. But I do not think it right for me or for anyone else to compel others to believe, especially not when this attempted compulsion is based on arguments which are logically contradictory. God does not expect us to believe in logical contradictions. Nonsense belongs best in fiction, with the Red Queen in *Alice* who could believe six impossible things before breakfast. There it is entertaining. In religious discussions, far from being entertaining, it is a nuisance and a dangerous nuisance at that.

Let us look more closely at the kind of things literalists and fundamentalists — those who believe the Bible to be true word for word — actually say. It is not fair to caricature their doctrine, so let us, wherever possible, quote their exact words. In the *New Bible Commentary* first published in 1953 and reprinted six times in as many years — so you can see how numerous the fundamentalists are — Dr J. I. Packer writes:

> Inspiration is . . . defined as a supernatural influence of God's Spirit upon the biblical authors which ensured that what they wrote was precisely what God intended them to write . . .

Since truth is communicated through words, and verbal inaccuracy misrepresents meaning, inspiration must be verbal in the nature of the case.

It is almost blasphemy to deny that it (the Bible) is free from error . . .

[And God did] So prepare and control the human instruments through whom he caused Scripture to be written that they put down exactly what he intended, no more and no less.

None of this is true and we can prove that it is not true simply by following James Barr's example and pointing to instances where the Bible contradicts itself. When the book Samuel gives different number of 'horsemen and foot' from the numbers given by the book Chronicles in the same battle then one account must be false. Logical contradictions are still logical contradictions even when they are connected with talk about God. And the particular goodness, niceness and friendliness of the speaker does not affect the argument one way of the other. I have no doubt that many literalists and fundamentalists are very good people and extremely nice to know but that doesn't mean that I am forced to believe any one of their doctrines when those doctrines are based on a contradiction. It cannot be both raining and not raining at the same time in one and the same place. A piece of material which is completely wood cannot be completely steel at the same time. And two contradictory descriptions of the same event cannot both be correct. It follows that one must be in error and therefore that the Bible is not true word for word. It may be true in parts or even true in a different sense but we shall return to this idea later.

How do the literalists know that the Bible is true in the way they suggest that it is true? F. A. Schaeffer in a book (perhaps not surprisingly) called *Escape from Reason* writes:

The Bible sets forth its own statement of what the Bible itself is. It presents itself as God's communication of propositional truth, written in verbalised form to those who are made in God's image.

This is a strange argument and you ought to be able to tell why it is not valid. It is invalid because it is an argument in a circle. It says in effect 'The Bible is true because the Bible says it is true because the Bible is true'. And this won't do at all, for any evidence as to the truth or falsity of a statement or set of statements must come from outside that statement or set of statements. To take an example off the subject. Suppose I say to you 'Here is the truth' and then go on to make a statement about something or other — about anything you like, a football score or the weather, it doesn't matter. My saying 'Here is the truth' adds nothing to what I allege to be the truth. Or, if you like, consider the value you would be likely to put on the reply, 'I always tell the truth' to your suspicion that the person in question might sometimes tell lies. Circular arguments lead nowhere.

There must be some external check. Some way of breaking into the circle. Otherwise no attempt to justify the statement first made succeeds when we argue in a circle. We are simply saying 'It's true because it's true', 'A = A', 'A man is a man' etc. The fact that in our case it is the authority of the Bible which is being used to defend the authority of the Bible makes no difference. It remains a pointless argument in a circle.

Another argument against literalism is the process of translation. Literalists usually quote the Bible in English or in the language which their hearers are most familiar with. Now if, as Dr Packer says '. . . the biblical authors wrote precisely what God intended them to write' then God must have intended the Old Testament in Hebrew and the New Testament in Greek because those were the languages in which they were originally written. This may seem a small point but listen to what J. B. Phillips in *Your God is Too Small* says on the subject:

> Although I believe in the true inspiration of the New Testament and its obvious power to change human lives in this or any other century, I should like to make it quite clear that I could not possibly hold the extreme 'fundamentalist' position of so called 'verbal inspiration'. This theory is bound to break down sooner or later in the world of translation.

J. B. Phillips goes on to talk about the difficulty of speaking to Eskimos of 'the true Vine' or 'the branches', or the tribes who have never seen water about 'an anchor for the soul'. More simple still is the fact that Greek has three or four words which it regularly uses for the English word 'love'. How then are we to convey the precise meaning of the original language in our own? This is not a small point for it is precise meanings about which the literalists claim to be so concerned. Again, as James Barr says:

> It seems to me only right that they be required to face facts of this kind. It is their doctrine, and not that of anyone else, that has made such sets of facts a problem. They have no right to say airily that they are not concerned about petty details.

It is necessary to spend this amount of time on the false doctrine of literalism since so often it is the only theory of revelation most people come into contact with. And because it is contradictory and false it does a grave injustice to Christianity. I do not wish to 'ram religion down peoples' throats' as I hope is clear by what I've written already in this book. But I am concerned that religion gets a fair hearing and is not dismissed as rubbish because of the false, if well-publicized, doctrines of cranks and fundamentalists. Often the literalist interpretation is all that the open-minded non-believer hears. Tragically, when he rightly dismisses it for the nonsense which it is, he dismisses the whole of Christianity with it for he mistakenly believes that literalism *is* Christianity. It is not.

It is also necessary to draw attention to the bigotry and intolerance of some literalists. J. I. Packer writes in *Fundamentalism and the Word of God:*

> Types of Christianity which regard as authoritative either tradition (as Romanism does) or reason (as liberalism does) are perversions of the faith.

Dr Packer and his associates must be told in the nicest possible way that this statement is false. The most obvious 'perversion of the faith' I have come across is literalism itself because it is based on a logical contradiction. God (if he exists) may ask us to believe in signs and wonders and miracles but no one — not even God, not even Dr Packer — should ask us to believe *both* of two contradictory descriptions of the same event. When you come to try and make sense of religion try to discount such outbursts as the following — also by Dr Packer in the same work:

> ... the evangelical principle of authority is authentically Christian, whereas other principles are not.
>
> Accordingly we shall contend that 'Fundamentalism' ... is in principle nothing but Christianity itself.

One final word on literalism. I have heard it said that although literalism is not true, one ought to teach it because it is easily understandable whereas other interpretations of Scripture are not. I reject this idea completely for two reasons. First, because I have more respect for the intelligence of young people than the literalists appear to have — or I wouldn't write a book like this about so called 'big' problems in the first place. And secondly, because I do not believe that where one cannot communicate complex facts one should instead teach simple fictions.

Biblical Revelation — The Wider Approach

Does the Bible reveal God to us in some other, non-literal way? A revelation of this kind is not disproved in advance by any logical principle. And certainly we should be wrong to think that only the knowledge which is gained through a completely literal understanding can be trusted. The literalists seem to want to make out that the Bible is like the timetable for some ideal railway company — everything happens exactly according to schedule, to the very dots and commas of the schedule, and there is no room for deviation to the right or to the left. But we sometimes claim to have learned truths by quite different methods. Everyone gets the message of Aesop's fable about the shepherd boy who cried wolf. It is not necessary to our understanding that Aesop should have been talking about an actual shepherd boy who really lived in order for us to profit from this story. Indeed, we may go so far as to say that the value of the fable would be neither increased nor decreased one bit even if there had never existed that particular shepherd boy.

In the same way, if one of our friends tells us about his visit to a horror film and says: 'I was frightened to death' we don't think he actually died. Obviously he didn't or he wouldn't be here to tell his tale! But we know what he means just the same. He means he was terrified. Sometimes it rains cats and dogs — or at least that's what folks say. When we were in the first year at school weren't we called 'chumps' and 'woodenheads'? What I'm trying to explain is, as you already know because you use language in this way, that there are many ways of speaking and writing knowledge in order to convey information. It's plainly wrong to think that the only way is via the literal account or list. There are myths, legends, parables, fables and metaphors. There is poetry as well as prose. Now, is it possible that the Bible uses words in these various ways? That it isn't simply a literal catalogue of unlikely events but a mixture of all kinds of literature, each kind valuable in its own way? Most present-day biblical scholars claim that this is just what the Bible is and that we should expect to find in it many different literary forms. Remembering that the Bible is not one book but sixty-six different and distinct volumes written over a period of about eight hundred years, let us have a look at some of these forms.

First we must realize that what we call 'the Bible' is further divided into two parts. The history of the Jewish people and their religious development is called the Old Testament. The stories about Jesus and the early church are called the New Testament. These two testaments or 'witnesses' are bound together in one book because Christians believe that the stories about Jesus are a completion of the Jewish writings. That God revealed himself first to Abraham, Isaac and Jacob and then in the fullness of time through his Son born in the world as Jesus of Nazareth and called by his followers 'Christ'. In other words, the Bible is all of a piece. It is one continuing story.

History

Some say that the word 'history' is the most boring word ever invented. Certainly it can be tedious when it's just a list of dates and battles but it can be interesting and exciting at times. In the Bible it is both. The stories about David and Solomon, about the fighting and the exile, about Jesus' life and the growth of the Christian community are lively and compelling reading. But you won't get much fun out of the Book of Leviticus (in the Old Testament) or out of some of the more tedious details of Paul's sailing plans (in the New Testament).

We must ask of the Bible's historical accounts: 'Are they true?' But before we can answer this question we need to try and understand the mind and motives of the biblical authors. They worked differently from modern historians in that they were hardly ever concerned about writing down exactly what happened. The details of historical events were of less importance to them than their overwhelming desire to show that God acted in the history of his people. This doesn't mean that biblical history is all lies made up to persuade gullible souls to believe in the Almighty God. It does mean that the biblical authors wrote from a particular point of view — from a firm belief that the people of Israel were specially chosen by God. When you think of it, modern history is not so different after all. Present-day historians are Conservatives, Liberals, Marxists etc. and they write from their own political persuasion. A Russian Communist historian is hardly likely to give the same account of the October Revolution as that given by a western Conservative. And this doesn't matter so long as we're aware that all history is written from a particular viewpoint and is bound to reflect to some extent the opinions and judgements of the writer. Once we understand a particular writer's point of view, his political allegiances or his religious presuppositions we can make suitable allowances. Someone once said that the only objective certainties in history are the dates of battles — and, if you go back far enough, even these are disputed! This doesn't mean that we can't trust the historians. Only that there are no such things as raw facts. All historical documents are interpretations of what happened.

Once we understand that the biblical historians were writing out of a deep faith in God we can take account of that fact in judging the worth of what they wrote. In the Old Testament the Books of Samuel, Kings and Chronicles are historical works written from this God-centred point of view. Take a few verses as a sample:

> Now these are the last words of David. David the Son of Jesse said, and the man who was raised up on high, the annointed of the God of Jacob, and the sweet psalmist of Israel said:
> 'The Spirit of the Lord spoke by me, and his word was in my tongue'.

You can see how God is as much a part of the scene as David, Jesse's son, the psalmist, Jacob etc. That's because the biblical historian could never imagine writing history which did not feature God strongly. A secular historian — one who does not automatically take a God-centred view — would have recorded the same event in a different way, perhaps simply saying: 'These are the last words of David who was once King of Israel'.

But for the biblical historian nothing happens unless it is caused or allowed by God. Throughout the Bible it is God who is said to 'summon up a mighty wind', to 'give his people victory in battle' and even to 'raise up enemies against his people'. There is a nice fancy word for this kind of writing. It's German so it's fun to pronounce and will remind you of the biblical writers' point of view: Heilsgeschichte — meaning 'holy stories' or 'sacred history'. Well then, is sacred history true?

It's generally reckoned that the books Samuel, Kings and Chronicles are a pretty good account of the history of the Jewish People — though written from their own point of view of course. As we have seen already, these books are not an absolutely accurate historical record. In places they contradict what is said elsewhere in the account. But they do give a fair outline of the history of Israel from the time of Saul to the period of the Exile. That is as far as the ordinary historical facts are concerned. It is true that Nebuchadnezzar, King of Babylon, sacked Jerusalem. Whether he did this according to the command of God or not is another matter. This is where we run across the biblical writer's God-centred history again. We can, if we wish, simply ignore all the references to God and try to read the biblical history as we might read the history of any ancient people. And we can probably expect a similar degree of accuracy among many accounts of the rise and fall of quite distinct nations. The orthodox Jew and the Christian, however, see an emerging pattern in history, a developing plan. And they believe this is God's plan. For them history is the stage on which God unfolds his purposes for mankind and the Bible, they claim, should always be read with this understanding.

Certainly, if we read the history of God's people, we can see a purpose and unity in the whole process. Whether that purpose and that unity really derives from God himself guiding history or whether it is no more than the particular historical 'slant' of the writers is left for the individual reader to decide. To take an example from an earlier chapter: there is little doubt that Jesus 'suffered under Pontius Pilate was crucified, dead and buried'. There is perhaps room for more discussion when we claim that 'he died for our sins'. The Bible cannot logically 'force' anyone to believe in God. But the nature of the Scriptures — and particularly the historical parts — is such that if you already have a belief in God then they are likely to speak to you of him.

Myth

Some parts of the Bible are not historical at all. They are mythological. And a myth is a poetic or an imaginative account of an unexplained mystery. Perhaps we know more these days about the origins of language than they knew in biblical times. But for the ancient biblical writer the only way he could account for the origin of all the different tongues was to make up the story of the Tower of Babel. You can read it in Genesis II. It's interesting to note that the *New English Bible* makes it quite plain that this tale is a myth or a fairy story by beginning it with the words 'Once upon a time'.

The creation stories are mythological. Ancient man was faced with the task of explaining where the first people came from. He didn't shirk this impossible task — it's worth mentioning that with all our scientific knowledge we're still not certain — he told a story. There's nothing basically dishonest about this. To the ancient mind the myth of God's Spirit brooding on the waters of chaos at the beginning of time (or in the Babylonian myth of Marduk slaying the dragon Tiamat) was as good an account as any of how things began. Here's a point to ponder: who's to say that in another thousand years our present-day notions about the nature and origin of the universe won't seem equally fanciful, childishly pictorial and mythological?

We must be careful always to distinguish between myth and history. The subject-matter of an historical record is at least partly to describe as accurately as we can what happened at a particular time in a particular place — at Hastings, say, in 1066. Usually, myth is a way of answering the big problems which recur generation after generation: why is there anything at all? How did we come to speak in languages? Misunderstanding has occurred in the discussion of religion, and the Bible in particular, when certain people have insisted mistakenly that the substance of myths actually happened on the surface of history. As we have seen, this led to a great deal of trouble and bitterness a hundred years ago when some religious leaders and teachers tried to insist in the literal historicity of the creation stories in Genesis in opposition to the theory of man's gradual evolution. This was very sad and did much damage to the church's image. We should try to avoid such misunderstandings in the future because there are enough problems in the discussion of religious matters without complicating the issue by talking at cross purposes.

Legend or Saga

You know the stories of King Arthur and the Knights of the Round Table. Everyone has read about Robin Hood. These are legends or examples of historical saga. That is to say they contain some historical truth but the original facts have been 'embroidered' to make the stories more interesting and compelling. Perhaps there was a King Arthur and it's almost certain there was a Robin Hood. But that doesn't mean we should regard as literally true all the stories which are told about them. They are folk heroes. Giants of the past. And we like nothing better than to romanticize about them. The tales of Abraham, Isaac and Jacob, the stories about Joseph and his coat of many colours; of Moses and the plagues of Egypt; of Samson and Delilah; David and Goliath are all examples of legend or saga. They contain some historical truth but they have gathered extra layers of colour and exaggeration as time has gone by.

These stories travelled for hundreds of years by word of mouth before they achieved a final written form. Generation after generation of Jewish children would sit at the feet of their fathers and by the side of the Old Man of the Tribe — the Patriarch — and hear these tales told and retold, subtly altered and added to by 'faith's imagination' over the years. It may be that the believer can see the inspiration of God even in the way these stories were exaggerated — putting flesh on the bare bones as it were. At the very least, they are stories of marvellous and everlasting interest as is shown for instance by the fact that *Joseph and his Amazing Technicoloured*

Dreamcoat was such a smash hit.

Jesus and the Gospel

But what about Jesus? This is the Bible story everybody knows. Was he
God's Son born of the Virgin Mary? Was he crucified dead and buried? Did
he rise again on the third day? And are we made fit for God and heaven
through what he did? How are we to take the New Testament's point of
view on this largest issue?

It is no simple question. It isn't even a single question but many. We
have discussed parts of it in earlier chapters in talking about miracles and
atonement but a full description of all the points involved would take up
many books — not just part of a single chapter in one short volume such as
this. Let us keep to what we do know beyond any reasonable doubt.

The first century A.D. saw the beginning of a new religious movement
called Christianity. From local origins it became the official religion of the
Roman Empire. It formed the cultural and spiritual point of reference for
the development of the western world for nineteen centuries. And it is still
influential. We are surely right to conclude that something pretty powerful
must have happened to generate this spiritual explosion. Perhaps what
happened was just exactly what the New Testament says happened — Jesus
was raised from the dead by God and his followers spent their lives spreading
the good news (Gospel), that through him men and women can lead a new
and exciting life (through the Holy Spirit) and eventually come to perfect
union with God in the life of the world to come.

Other Christian writers put a different interpretation on the biblical
account of the life, death and resurrection of Jesus. They claim that he was so
godly that it was appropriate to give him the title Son of God. Even that
he was the Messiah, the Promised One, expected by the Jews for centuries.
That he taught the way of love and personal fulfilment through self
sacrifice. He was misunderstood and finally, mistaken for a rebel, put to
death by the Roman Garrison in Judea. But that all did not come to an
end with his death. His disciples came to realize the truth of what Jesus
had been telling them while he was still with them. This had a profound
influence upon them and changed the quality of their lives to such an
extent that they could only express the depth of their new-found joy in
the proclamation 'Jesus is Risen'.

Which of these accounts do you find most convincing? Is there, perhaps,
even another version of the facts, one I haven't mentioned because I
don't know about it? Those who believe the biblical record as it stands
simply don't believe that Christianity could have got off the ground as a
religious movement unless Jesus had risen from the dead. The disciples
would have remained the same frightened men who deserted Jesus at the
time of his arrest. What could possibly have changed their minds and lives
except that God raised Jesus from the dead and he was revealed to them

on the first Easter Day?

Those Christians who hold the second theory do so out of a belief that the New Testament account is a mythological way of stating that a new quality of life is available in the here and now if we live as Jesus commanded. They argue that the account was necessarily mythological because men of the first century could not express spiritual truth in any other way. They had to describe their experience of new life by saying that Jesus had risen from the dead. What do you think? One thing is not in doubt, remember, and that is the fact of Christianity as a world-wide phenomenon. I can think of no better way to end this section than by quoting some famous words in the form of a question by Professor L. Hodgson:

> What must the truth be, and have been, if it appeared like that to men who thought and wrote as they did?

Summary

At the beginning of this chapter we tried to understand the meaning of the word 'revelation' and then looked at some of the problems surrounding it. We did at least achieve the negative result of showing what revelation cannot possibly be — a word for word (literal) inspiration by God of the very words of Scripture. We are able to prove this because we saw that in certain places the Bible offers more than one account of the same incident and sometimes these accounts contradict each other. Therefore they cannot both be correct. We moved on to look at the question of revelation in the wider context of an understanding of the forms of biblical literature — history, saga, myth and proclamation. We see that we cannot be certain of whether the Bible is a revelation of God's purposes for his people and his universe or whether it is not simply the personal opinions of a particular group of religious writers.

We conclude by noting three indisputable facts:

(1) The Bible can reinforce and strengthen belief when that belief is already there.

(2) The Bible can convince men and women of the reality of God. Many have been so convinced simply by reading it.

(3) Many other people, equally honest, have felt obliged to turn away from the Bible, respecting its literary merits, but sceptical of its contents.

Exercises

(1) If there is revelation, why doesn't God reveal himself to everyone?

(2) What is the 'keep off the grass' theory of revelation? Do you find it convincing?

(3) How could we ever know for certain that an alleged revelation was a revelation in fact?

(4) If God reveals himself through the Christian tradition, does that mean all other religions are false?

(5) What is wrong with the doctrine of the literal (word for word) inspiration of Scripture? How can we prove this to be wrong?

(6) What is meant by arguing 'in a circle'? Invent one or two examples.

(7) Explain the difference between history, myth and saga.

(8) Divide into groups. Let each group invent its own mythological explanation of the origin of the universe.

(9) Did Jesus rise from the dead? If so, how could such a thing be possible? If not, what changed the disciples from frightened men into enthusiasts for the Gospel?

(10) Has God ever revealed himself to you, directly? Prove it.

7 Epilogue

In one sense we've got nowhere at all in this book. We were unable to prove the existence of God. Unsure about heaven. Puzzled at the idea of miracles. Not certain how to judge the claims of religion and science. Unable to account for evil and baffled by the problems surrounding revelation.

In another sense we can perhaps claim some small success for we have tried to enter the discussion about some of the largest problems which confront mankind and which have occupied the best minds for centuries. You might say we've had a close encounter of a worthwhile theological kind.

At the end we've proved nothing — except that one or two ideas about religion in general and about the Bible in particular are misleading because false. And yet I don't think we've been wasting our time. I don't know whether there is a God but I choose to believe that there is. My reasons for this belief may not seem to amount to much and I know that they can each be dismissed one by one. Indeed we have spent a good deal of time and space in these chapters doing quite a bit of 'dismissing' on our own account. But at the end I am forced, or so it seems to me, to choose between God and a universe of blind chance. Between some kind of order or purpose and a vast randomness of one damned thing after another. I believe in God simply because it seems to me more likely that there is some reason for the universe — that it's not an accident. What I mean is that if I stand the argument on its head and try not to believe in God then I have more problems than I had when I tried to believe in him. Bacon's words come back to mind:

> I had rather believe all the fables in the Legend and the Talmud, and the Alcoran, than that this universal frame is without a mind . . .

The universe is quite simply so staggeringly large, varied and beautiful, so utterly mysterious, constantly revealing new truths, new aspects of itself that I cannot bring myself to believe that it just is and that's all there is to it. Of course, I am frequently beset by doubt, when I feel as if I'm just willing myself to believe because the alternative would be despair. But whenever I persevere in trying not to believe I find that in the end I'm forced, almost unwillingly, to come to the conclusion that there simply must be something or someone behind and in all this wonder. I don't know whether this makes me a good Christian or a bad one but it is what I feel bound to believe in the light of ordinary experience.

One verse in the Bible has God saying 'Behold I make all things new'. And it is this newness of things which encourages my belief. There are always new marvels in the arts and sciences. After the wonder of *Don Giovanni* there was still the *Magic Flute* to come. What next? Beethoven, Mahler, Schoenberg. After Michaelangelo and Leonardo art did not come to a stop. But instead Velasquez, Picasso, Klee, Kandinsky — the list never ends. Shakespeare, Goethe, Hopkins, Eliot, Joyce . . .

We know that strictly speaking it's impossible to prove the occurrence of miracles, but where does this list of wonders ever cease? There was the old bush telegraph then flashing lights, morse and semaphore. But one day, behold, radio was invented. Television. Space travel, lasers, holons. What next?

I know these things can all be put down to the works of men's hands and that they do not prove there must be a creative mind directing the universe. But I ask myself which seems more plausible, that these wonders are all just lucky accidents, that the joy which new wonders of discovery brings is a biological hiccup in a materialist's universe, or that they are the result of the operation of God's creative spirit? I am obliged to choose the second explanation. Physicists tell us that the universe seems to be made out of 'mind' stuff rather than 'matter' stuff. The movements of the fundamental particles — which aren't particles at all really but units of high energy — cannot be individually predicted. All we can do is generalize statistically about the structure of 'non-material matter'. What price the nineteenth-century's materialistic and deterministic universe now in the age of 'the quark' and 'charm'? Besides, if the universe is more like mind stuff than material stuff then doesn't that suggest that it's someone's idea? And may we not call that someone 'God'? The old view of the universe as some kind of machine that operates according to fixed mechanical laws is no longer tenable. Arthur Koestler writes colourfully in his book *The Roots of Coincidence*:

> We have heard a whole chorus of Nobel Laureates in physics informing us that matter is dead, causality is dead, determinism is dead. If that is so, let us give them a decent burial with a requiem of electronic music. It is time for us to draw the lessons from 20th century post-mechanistic science, and to get out of the straight jacket which 19th century materialism imposed on our philosophical outlook. Paradoxically, had that outlook kept abreast with modern science itself, instead of lagging a century behind it, we should have been liberated from that straight jacket long ago.

In my opinion the present century is revealing to us a universe wonderful beyond our wildest flights of fantasy. I reckon there is something behind it. Perhaps the word 'God' is not a very useful one, conjuring up as it does old superstitions. But what other word shall we use? 'Meaning'? 'Purpose'? That old film *Star Wars* spoke of 'The Force'. The people of Israel wouldn't pronounce God's name at all. I'm not particularly worried what name we choose to refer to that something or someone who is responsible for the wonders of the universe. But I am unable to believe that he (or she or it) is merely a product of my imagination or a piece of wishful thinking. It is, to me, incredible that there should be all this and no God.

The Persistence of Evil

But I have to face the unpleasant fact of the dark side of the universe. Pain and suffering. Torture and sudden death. Earthquakes, floods and famines. These are not easily explained away. In fact I think that most attempted solutions of the problem of evil fail miserably to square up to the terrible as well as to the beautiful facts of life.

In my opinion it will not do to say 'These things are sent to try us' or 'It'll all be alright in the end' or 'Evil is not really real; it's just an absence of good'. I think evil is absolutely real, that it is a mystery not to be explained away by utilitarian theologies of 'the best of all possible worlds' variety or by theories of the atonement which remind one more of accountancy than divinity.

After all his advisers had finished trying to explain evil to Job I think he got the only answer it is possible to receive when, as the Old Testament writer says, the Lord answered him out of the whirlwind:

> Who is this that darkeneth counsel by words without knowledge . . .
> Where wast thou when I laid the foundations of the earth? . . .
> when the morning stars sang together and all the sons of God shouted
> for joy . . . where is the way where light dwelleth, and as for darkness
> where is the place thereof? . . .

In other words the Almighty God is beyond our definitions of good and evil. His ways are above our ways and we can never expect to understand him completely. We are creatures but he is our creator. The best translation of the Hebrew word for God: *Yahweh* — often rendered 'I am' — is 'I will be who I will be'. Jesus said to Nicodemus 'The Spirit blows where it wills'. God is God and that's that.

If we do choose to believe in God, and it's a free choice for everyone, we cannot simply expect to create God in our own image or invent a God whom we could wish might exist. Belief in God means acceptance of God as he is and not how we would prefer him to be. All our language about him then becomes symbolic. As Goethe wrote: 'All transitory things are as but symbols sent'.

We cannot expect God to conform to the definitions of human philosophizing. He is God and we are men. He is infinite and we are limited. He is from everlasting. We are mortal. Once we commit ourselves to a belief in God then all our reasoning must take second place to that commitment. Which is not to say that we should lapse into faulty logic and bad arguments only that as Kierkegaard said:

> It is one thing to stand on one leg and prove God's existence: quite another to fall to our knees and worship him.

There is no compulsion to believe in God. You are at liberty to disagree with me and say that belief is not for you. There is nothing illogical or unreasonable about that. It is neither a sinful nor an immoral point of view to take. But if you do decide that there is a God then your attitude towards him must change from that of armchair philosophizing to adoration and worship. You can't carry the belief in God around with you as an optional extra like fire insurance. That is to caricature God. It is to worship an idol. Perhaps I am not hopelessly deceived when I claim that this strange God who is beyond definition, who answers Job out of the whirlwind, who 'will be who he will be' and who allows evil in his universe, has spoken to us in the life and death of his Son Jesus Christ. And that the way in which we can draw near him was also pointed out by his Son: by faith. By loving one another. By loving our enemies!

R. C. Zaehner (putting words into the mouth of Jesus) writes:

> I Jesus, the Son of Mary, can do this because my father and 'form' is God: my father has killed me because I am his second self. He has killed himself. But he cannot die because he is pure, unchanging . . . I can: because the Matter that made it possible for me to become a social animal at all I took from my Mother Mary who willingly accepted the common lot of our chosen Jewish race which is to kiss the hand that strikes us . . . She accepted everything on your behalf because she was the kind of silly little child I love. You can do the same, but only with my help.

What do you think?

Further Reading

Chapters

5	—	Aulen, G. *Christus Victor* (SPCK)
6	—	Barr, J. *Fundamentalism* (SCM)
6	—	Barth, K. *The Faith of the Church* (Fontana)
7	—	Berger, P.L. *A Rumour of Angels* (Pelican)
7	—	Berkeley, G. *The Principles of Human Knowledge* (Fontana)
2	—	Black, M. (ed) *Peake's Commentary on the Bible* (Nelson)
1 & 5	—	Bonhoeffer, D. *Letters and Papers from Prison* (Fontana)
6	—	Bultmann, R. *Primitive Christianity* (Fontana)
6	—	Butterfield, H. *Christianity and History* (Fontana)
2	—	Cavendish, R. *Visions of Heaven and Hell* (Orbis)
7	—	Chesterton, G.K. *Orthodoxy* (Fontana)
4	—	Coulson, C.A. *Science and Christian Belief* (Fontana)
1	—	Flew, A. (ed) *Body, Mind and Death* (MacMillan)
4	—	Flew, A. and MacIntyre, A. (ed) *New Essays in Philosophical Theology* (SCM)
1	—	Healey, F. G. *Fifty Keywords in Theology* (Lutterworth)
1 & 5	—	Hick, J. *Evil and the God of Love* (Fontana)
1	—	Hick, J. and McGill, A. (ed) *The Many Faced Argument* (MacMillan)
1	—	Hume, D. *Dialogues* (Fontana)
3	—	Hume, D. *Enquiry Concerning the Human Understanding* (Oxford)
2	—	James, E.O. *Comparative Religion* (Penguin)
7	—	James, W. *Varieties of Religious Experience* (Fontana)
7	—	Koestler, A. *The Roots of Coincidence* (Picador)
3	—	Lewis, C.S. *Miracles* (Fontana)
5	—	Lewis, C.S. *The Problem of Pain* (Fontana)
1	—	MacGregor, G. *Introduction to Religious Philosophy* (MacMillan)
7	—	Mullen, P. *Beginning Philosophy* (Edward Arnold)
6	—	Nineham, D.E. *St Mark* (Penguin)
6	—	Packer, J.I. (ed) *New Bible Commentary* (IVP)
6	—	Packer, J.I. *Fundamentalism and the Word of God* (IVP)
6	—	Parmalee, A. *A Guidebook to the Bible* (English Universities Press)

Chapters

2 — Pascal, B. *Pensees* (Everyman)

6 — Phillips, J.B. *Your God is Too Small* (Wyvern)

3 — Pike, R. *Around The Year With The World's Religions* (Watts and Co.)

4 — Pilkington, R. *World Without End* (Fontana)

6 — Quick, O.C. *Doctrines of the Creed* (Fontana)

1 — Ramsey, I. (ed) *Words About God* (SCM)

3 — Ramsey, I. (ed) *The Miracles and the Resurrection* (SPCK)

6 — Rein, G. (ed) *A New Look at the Apostles' Creed* (St Andrew)

6 — Schaeffer, F.A. *Escape from Reason* (IVP)

5 — Schopenhauer, F. *Essays and Aphorisms* (Penguin)

7 — Smart, N. *Philosophers and Religious Truth* (SCM)

1 — Taylor, A.E. *Does God Exist?* (Fontana)

2 — Watson, D. *My God is Real* (Falcon)

7 — Wisdom, J. *Problems of Mind and Matter* (Cambridge)

7 — Zaehner, R.C. *Drugs, Mysticism and Make-believe* (Collins)